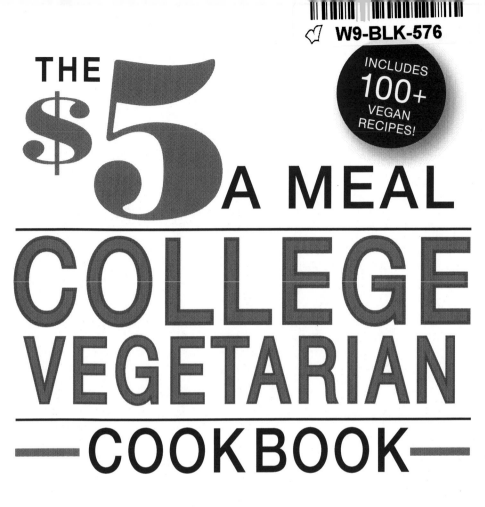

INCLUDES **100+** VEGAN RECIPES!

W9-BLK-576

THE $5 A MEAL

COLLEGE VEGETARIAN

—COOKBOOK—

Good, cheap vegetarian recipes
for when you need to eat

NICOLE CORMIER, RD, LDN

Aadamsmedia
Avon, Massachusetts

Published by
Adams Media, a division of F+W Media, Inc.
57 Littlefield Street, Avon, MA 02322. U.S.A.
www.adamsmedia.com

Contains portions of material adapted and abridged from *The Everything® Vegan Cookbook*,
by Jolinda Hackett with Lorena Novak Bull, RD, copyright © 2010 by F+W Media, Inc., ISBN
10: 1-4405-0216-1; ISBN 13: 978-1-4405-0216-3; *The Everything® Vegetarian Cookbook*, by
Jay Weinstein, copyright © 2002 by F+W Media, Inc., ISBN 10: 1-5806-2640-8; ISBN-13: 978-
1-58062-640-8; *The Everything® College Cookbook*, by Rhonda Lauret Parkinson, copyright
© 2005 by F+W Media, Inc., ISBN 10: 1-59337-303-1; ISBN 13: 978-1-59337-303-0; and
The $5 a Meal College Cookbook, by Rhonda Lauret Parkinson and B. E. Horton, MS, RD,
copyright © 2010 by F+W Media, Inc., ISBN 10: 1-4405-0208-0; ISBN 13: 978-1-4405-0208-8.

ISBN 10: 1-4405-5267-3
ISBN 13: 978-1-4405-5267-0
eISBN 10: 1-4405-5268-1
eISBN 13: 978-1-4405-5268-7

Printed in the United States of America.

10 9 8 7 6 5 4 3 2 1

Always follow safety and common-sense cooking protocol while using kitchen utensils,
operating ovens and stoves, and handling uncooked food. If children are assisting in the
preparation of any recipe, they should always be supervised by an adult.

This book is available at quantity discounts for bulk purchases.
For information, please call 1-800-289-0963.

Contents

Introduction

Pizza. Spaghetti. Peanut butter sandwiches. Does this sound an awful lot like your vegetarian menu when you're away at college?

College is an adventure. It's a time filled with new people, a new environment, and many exciting experiences. But heading off for college can present challenges as well as opportunities—especially when it comes to food. Sure, there might be a ton of bread, pasta, and rice available, but it can be difficult to create a nutritionally complete meal with the ingredients that you find in your college dining hall—especially when you're eating on a college student's budget.

Fortunately, in *The $5 a Meal College Vegetarian Cookbook* you'll find more than 300 easy-to-make recipes that will keep your vegetarian diet on track whether you're looking to start your day with a delicious Apple and Cinnamon Muffin (see Chapter 1), chow down on some Easy Eggplant Parmigiana (see Chapter 7) for dinner, or enjoy some Italian Pesto Popcorn (see Chapter 3) during a late-night study break. And, in addition to the vegetarian recipes found throughout, you'll also find a variety of vegan recipes like French Fries from Scratch (see Chapter 3), Three-Bean Salad (see Chapter 4), and Foolproof Vegan Fudge (see Chapter 8). You can find these vegan recipes by looking for the **Ⓥ** callout throughout. You'll also find that each recipe has nutritional stats included so you'll always know exactly what you're eating—a rarity in the college world of cheap take-out and late-night snack fests.

And if you're worried that you won't be able to afford eating a vegetarian diet on a college student's budget, think again! Every single serving found in this book costs less than $5—some significantly so!—so you can keep your hard-earned work-study money where it belongs—in your wallet!

So put down your textbook and pick up a skillet. It's time to get cooking—vegetarian-style!

Getting Started

Yes, healthy, homemade vegetarian food is within your grasp—and within your cooking ability!—but you can't cook if you don't have the supplies. What do you need? Well, what you should stock up on depends on your specific circumstances. Do you live in a dorm with a communal kitchen that provides pots, pans, and other cooking essentials for students? Do you live in an off-campus apartment? No matter your situation, most of the essentials are inexpensive and can usually be found at discount stores—and a few basic items will go a long way.

KITCHEN SUPPLIES

To start out, you want to make sure that you have the kitchen supplies that you need to actually make the vegetarian and vegan dishes that you love. Again, you can buy a lot of these supplies cheap, and it's much better to just buy them all in advance, rather than running out late at night when you just *have* to have Mini Goat Cheese Pizzas (see Chapter 3) or a serving of No-Bake Cocoa Balls (see Chapter 8). So to avoid some sort of a food emergency, make sure you have the following on hand:

- Can opener
- Cleaver (knife)
- Grater
- Heatproof rubber spatula
- Measuring spoons and measuring cup
- Metal colander
- Plastic mixing bowls for mixing ingredients and serving dishes
- Vegetable peeler
- Wire whisk
- Wooden or bamboo cutting board
- Wooden or bamboo spoon
- Zester

In addition, if there's room in your budget—and your dorm or student residence permits them—there are some basic electrical appliances that may come in handy:

- Coffeemaker
- Food processor
- Hot plate and/or rice cooker
- Microwave
- Toaster or toaster oven

Once you've purchased the basic tools needed for cooking, you may want to purchase containers for portioning out individual meals. This way, one recipe will provide you with multiple meals. A little time in the kitchen could feed you all week long—and, with all the time you'll spend cramming for exams and hanging out with your friends, anything that can save you time in the kitchen is a very good thing.

STOCK YOUR PANTRY

You'll need to read through each recipe before deciding what fresh ingredients you need to buy, but that doesn't mean that you can't stock your pantry with dry ingredients and some canned foods for quick meals. Try loading up on these vegetarian essentials:

Baking Goods
- All-purpose flour
- Sugar (raw)
- Unsweetened cocoa powder
- Whole-wheat flour

Beans (Canned or Dried)
- Adzuki
- Black
- Black-eyed peas
- Butter
- Cannellini
- Chickpeas
- Dried lentils
- Kidney
- Pinto

Dried Herbs and Spices
- Basil
- Bay leaf
- Cayenne pepper
- Cinnamon
- Coriander
- Cumin
- Curry
- Fresh ground pepper
- Garlic powder
- Ginger
- Nutritional yeast
- Oregano
- Parsley
- Rosemary
- Sea salt
- Whole-wheat pasta

Flavorings

- Apple cider vinegar
- Balsamic vinegar
- Dijon mustard
- Honey
- Lemon juice
- Rice vinegar
- Soy sauce or tamari
- Tomato sauce

Grains

- Brown rice
- Buckwheat
- Quinoa
- Rolled oats
- Wheat berries

Oils

- Coconut oil
- Olive oil
- Peanut oil
- Sesame seed oil

Once you have the basics, you're ready to start cooking! So say goodbye to peanut butter and jelly sandwiches and pasta from the dining hall and hello to delicious vegetarian meals that fill you up without emptying your wallet! Enjoy!

CHAPTER 1

Breakfasts

You've heard a million times that breakfast is the most important meal of the day, and it's true! Breakfast starts your metabolism and sets the tone for managing your blood sugars, energy levels, and hunger throughout the day. But if breakfast is so important, why is it so hard to make sure you're actually eating it?

For starters, after a late-night study session it can be hard to get up early for an 8 A.M. class just to make sure you're starting your day off right! But it doesn't have to be that way. This chapter gives you a variety of recipes to choose from. Some you can make in advance so all you have to do is grab and go as you head to class. Some are perfect for lazy Saturday and Sunday mornings when you're looking for something a little more substantial. But all are absolutely delicious and, at less than $5 a serving, can't be beat!

Basic Bagel with Cream Cheese

Serves 2

COST: $0.60

For ½ bagel
Calories: 220
Fat: 7g
Carbohydrates: 31g
Protein: 7g
Fiber: 3g
Sugar: 2g
Sodium: 327mg

1 bagel, any flavor (whole grain is healthiest)
2 teaspoons raisins
2 teaspoons chopped walnuts

2 tablespoons plain cream cheese
½ teaspoon (or to taste) ground cinnamon

1. Cut the bagel in half and place in toaster. While the bagel is toasting, chop the raisins.
2. Mix together the raisins, walnuts, and cream cheese. Stir in the ground cinnamon. Spread the cream cheese mixture on the toasted bagel.

Serving Note

This recipe makes enough for 2 breakfasts and is best served with a piece of fruit or 1 cup of fruit. You will get the most out of your breakfast by incorporating a protein, whole grain, and at least 1 cup of fruit or 1 piece. Each fruit has a unique composition of vitamins, minerals, and fiber that support your energy levels and health.

Garlic Cheese Toast

Serves 1

COST: $0.64 PER 2 SLICES
Calories: 277
Fat: 12g
Carbohydrates: 33g
Protein: 9g
Fiber: 4g
Sugar: 2.5g
Sodium: 460mg

2 teaspoons butter
2 small slices rye bread

¼ teaspoon garlic powder
2 tablespoons ricotta cheese

1. Spread the butter on the bread. Mix the garlic powder into the ricotta cheese and spread onto the bread.
2. Broil in the oven until the toast is lightly browned and the cheese is softened (but not completely melted). Serve warm.

Ⓥ Quick and Easy Vegan Biscuits

Yields 12 biscuits

COST: $0.12
Per biscuit
Calories: 123
Fat: 5g
Carbohydrates: 16g
Protein: 3g
Fiber: 1g
Sugar: 0g
Sodium: 211mg

2 cups flour
1 tablespoon baking powder
½ teaspoon onion powder
½ teaspoon garlic powder
½ teaspoon salt

5 tablespoons cold vegan margarine
⅔ cup unsweetened soy milk

1. Preheat oven to 425°F.
2. Combine flour, baking powder, onion powder, garlic powder, and salt in a large bowl. Add margarine.
3. Using a fork, mash the margarine with the dry ingredients until crumbly.
4. Add soy milk a few tablespoons at a time and combine just until dough forms. You may need to add a little more or less than ⅔ cup.
5. Knead a few times on a floured surface, then roll out to ¾ inch thick. Cut into 3-inch rounds.
6. Bake for 12–14 minutes, or until the tops are lightly browned.

Berry English Muffins

Serves 4

COST: $1.61

Per English muffin
Calories: 278
Fat: 13g
Carbohydrates: 32g
Protein: 7g
Fiber: 3g
Sugar: 4g
Sodium: 352mg

4 English muffins
2 teaspoons lemon juice
8 tablespoons plain cream cheese

1 cup blueberries
2 tablespoons walnuts

1. Split the English muffins in half and toast. While the muffins are toasting, stir the lemon juice into the cream cheese, mashing to mix it in thoroughly. Then fold in blueberries.
2. Spoon a heaping tablespoon of the mixture onto each toasted muffin half. Top with ½ tablespoon of walnuts.

Ⓥ Apricot Applesauce

Yields 4 cups

COST: $1.15

Per ½ cup
Calories: 89
Fat: 0g
Carbohydrates: 23g
Protein: 1g
Fiber: 2.5g
Sugar: 19g
Sodium: 1mg

6 apples
⅓ cup water
½ cup dried apricots, chopped

4 dates, chopped
Cinnamon to taste

1. Peel, core, and chop apples. Add apples and water to a large soup or stockpot and bring to a low boil. Simmer, covered, for 15 minutes, stirring occasionally.
2. Add chopped apricots and dates and simmer for another 10–15 minutes.
3. Mash with a large fork until desired consistency is reached, or allow to cool slightly and purée in a blender until smooth. Sprinkle with cinnamon to taste if desired.

Hard-Boiled Eggs

Serves 2

COST: $0.28

Per egg
Calories: 71
Fat: 4g
Carbohydrates: 0.5g
Protein: 7g
Fiber: 0g
Sugar: 0g
Sodium: 70mg

2 eggs, any size

1. Place the eggs in a saucepan and cover with cold water to at least ½ inch above the eggs. Cover the pan with the lid and bring to a rolling boil over high heat.
2. As soon as the water is boiling, remove from heat. Let the eggs stand in the hot water for 17–20 minutes.
3. Remove the eggs from the saucepan and place in a bowl filled with cold water for at least 2 minutes, or until cool enough to handle. Peel off the shells. The eggs will keep in the refrigerator for about 1 week.

Cage-Free, Farm Fresh, or Industrial

Farm fresh eggs are most nutritious due to their freshness and supply more vitamin A, vitamin E, and omega-3 fatty acids compared to industrial eggs. If you can't find farm fresh eggs near you, you can still buy cage-free eggs in the supermarket.

Soft-Boiled Eggs

Serves 2

COST: $0.28
Per egg
Calories: 71
Fat: 4g
Carbohydrates: 0.5g
Protein: 7g
Fiber: 0g
Sugar: 0g
Sodium: 70mg

2 eggs, any size

1. Fill a pot with enough cold water so that there will be at least ½ inch of water above the eggs. Bring the water to a rolling boil. Place the eggs in the pot and cook for 3–5 minutes (depending on your personal preference for soft-boiled eggs).
2. Remove the eggs from the pot and place in cold water until cool enough to handle. Peel off the shells. The eggs will keep in the refrigerator for up to 1 week.

Basic Poached Egg

Serves 2

COST: $0.28
Per egg
Calories: 71
Fat: 4g
Carbohydrates: 0.5g
Protein: 7g
Fiber: 0g
Sugar: 0g
Sodium: 70mg

2 eggs, any size

1. In a medium-sized saucepan, bring 3 inches of water to a boil. Add the salt to help the water boil faster. While waiting for the water to boil, break each egg into its own small bowl.
2. When the water reaches a boil, turn the heat down until it is just simmering. Gently slide the eggs into the simmering water and cook for 3–5 minutes, depending on how firm you like the yolk.
3. Remove the eggs with a slotted spoon, letting any excess water drain into the saucepan. Use the slotted spoon to gently push aside any "threads" from the egg white.

Perfect Scrambled Eggs

Serves 1

COST: $0.38
Per 2 eggs
Calories: 131
Fat: 11g
Carbohydrates: 1g
Protein: 7g
Fiber: 0g
Sugar: 1g
Sodium: 77mg

2 eggs
2 tablespoons milk
Salt and pepper, to taste

Paprika, to taste
1 tablespoon butter

1. Break the eggs into a small bowl. Add the milk, salt and pepper, and paprika.
2. Beat the eggs until they are an even color throughout.
3. In a small skillet, melt the butter over low heat. Increase heat to medium low and add the eggs.
4. Cook the eggs, using a spatula to turn sections of the egg from time to time so that the uncooked egg on top flows underneath. Adjust the heat as needed. For best results, remove the scrambled eggs from the pan when they are firm but still a bit moist (about 6–8 minutes).

Simple Eggs Benedict

Serves 1

COST: $0.89
Per English muffin
Calories: 320
Fat: 17g
Carbohydrates: 28g
Protein: 12g
Fiber: 2g
Sugar: 2g
Sodium: 409mg

1 English muffin
1 tablespoon butter
2 tablespoons plain yogurt
1 teaspoon prepared mustard

1 Basic Poached Egg (see recipe in this chapter)

1. Split the English muffin in half, toast, and butter both halves.
2. Mix together the yogurt and mustard.
3. Spread the yogurt and mustard mixture on one muffin half, and place the poached egg on the other half.

Miso Eggs Benedict

Serves 4

COST: $0.99

Per ½ English muffin
Calories: 400
Fat: 33g
Carbohydrates: 14g
Protein: 11g
Fiber: 1g
Sugar: 0.5g
Sodium: 829mg

3 tablespoons white vinegar
1 teaspoon salt
4 extra-large eggs
2 English muffins, split
½ teaspoon miso paste

½ cup hollandaise sauce
Chives
Hot pepper sauce

1. Combine the vinegar and salt in a deep skillet with 2 inches of water; bring to boil. Crack each egg into its own cup. When water boils, lower flame as low as you can. Gently lower the eggs into the hot water, one by one, and pour them from the cups into the pan. Toast the muffins.
2. Poach the eggs for no more than 3 minutes, then remove them with a slotted spoon, allowing excess water to drain back into the skillet. Transfer poached eggs to a waiting plate.
3. Spread miso onto the toasted muffins.
4. Place 1 poached egg onto each muffin half. Spoon generous helpings of hollandaise sauce onto each, and serve immediately with a sprinkling of chives and hot pepper sauce on the side.

Make It in Advance

Eggs can be poached up to a day in advance and stored submerged in cold water. To reheat, gently place in fresh boiling water for a minute before using. Serve this recipe with 1 cup of pineapple or other fruit for a complete breakfast.

Savory Scrambled Eggs

Serves 1

COST: $1.94

Per 2 eggs
Calories: 189
Fat: 17g
Carbohydrates: 2g
Protein: 7g
Fiber: 1g
Sugar: 2g
Sodium: 80mg

2 eggs
2 tablespoons milk
Salt and pepper, to taste
10 capers

2 tablespoons butter, divided
½ tomato, chopped
1 green onion, chopped

1. Break the eggs into a small bowl. Add the milk, salt and pepper, and capers. Beat until the eggs are an even color throughout.
2. In a small frying pan, melt 1 tablespoon butter on low heat.
3. Add the tomato and green onion. Cook until the tomato is tender but still firm. Remove from pan and set aside. Clean the pan.
4. Melt the remaining 1 tablespoon butter in the pan on low heat.
5. Turn the heat up to medium-low and add the eggs. Cook the eggs, using a spatula to turn sections of the egg from time to time so that the uncooked egg on top flows underneath. Adjust the heat up or down as needed to cook the eggs.
6. When the eggs are nearly cooked, return the tomato and green onion to the pan. Cook the scrambled eggs until they are firm but still a bit moist (about 6–8 minutes).

Huevos Rancheros

Serves 4

COST: $1.83

Per 2 tortillas
Calories: 308
Fat: 15g
Carbohydrates: 27g
Protein: 16g
Fiber: 6g
Sugar: 4g
Sodium: 666mg

1 can Mexican-style black
  beans in sauce
2 cups salsa
8 large eggs
½ cup half-and-half
Unsalted butter

8 soft corn tortillas (8-inch
  diameter)
1 cup shredded Cheddar
  cheese
½ cup sour cream
Chopped cilantro

1. Heat the beans and salsa in separate pots over low flames. Scramble together the eggs, and half-and-half. Melt the butter in a nonstick pan; cook the scrambled eggs over a low flame until soft and creamy, with small curds.
2. Soften the tortillas either by steaming or putting them in the microwave for 15 seconds. Place 2 tortillas onto each plate. Divide the hot black beans evenly onto these tortillas.
3. Spoon the eggs onto the beans, then sauce with a ladleful of salsa. Garnish with cheese, sour cream, and cilantro. Serve immediately.

Pair It with Protein

If you choose a refined carbohydrate for breakfast, but don't pair it with a protein, your body is then required to do its best to manage this high level of sugar in your blood. Unfortunately, the pancreas overworks itself leading to an excess of insulin and low blood sugars. This results in your body craving another quick source of energy throughout the rest of the day, creating a roller coaster effect.

Scrambled Eggs Masala

Serves 2

COST: $1.47

Per 2 eggs
Calories: 259
Fat: 21g
Carbohydrates: 4g
Protein: 13g
Fiber: 1g
Sugar: 2g
Sodium: 145mg

2 tablespoons butter
¼ cup chopped onion
¼ teaspoon cumin seed, toasted in a dry pan and crushed

¼ cup diced tomato
4 eggs, scrambled
Salt and white pepper to taste
4 teaspoons chopped fresh mint leaves (for garnish)

1. Melt the butter in a medium nonstick skillet over a moderate heat. Add the onion; cook 5–8 minutes, until soft. Add cumin and tomato; cook 1 minute more.
2. Stir in the eggs and salt and pepper. Using a wooden spoon, constantly stir the eggs until they form soft, creamy curds; transfer to plates and serve immediately. Garnish with the mint.

Basic Cheese Omelet

Serves 1

COST: $0.78

Per omelet
Calories: 308
Fat: 31g
Carbohydrates: 3g
Protein: 21g
Fiber: 6g
Sugar: 2g
Sodium: 340mg

2 eggs
2 tablespoons milk
Salt and pepper, to taste
¼ teaspoon (or to taste) chili powder

1 tablespoon butter
¼ cup grated cheese

1. Lightly beat the eggs with the milk. Stir in the salt, pepper, and chili powder. Melt the butter in a frying pan over low heat. Swirl the butter around to coat the pan entirely.
2. Pour the egg mixture into the pan. Cook over low heat. After the omelet has been cooking for a few minutes, sprinkle the grated cheese over half of the omelet. Tilt the pan occasionally or lift the edges of the omelet with a spatula so that the uncooked egg runs underneath.
3. When the omelet is cooked evenly throughout, loosen the edges of the omelet with a spatula. Carefully slide the spatula underneath the omelet and fold it in half. Slide the omelet onto a plate.

Boursin Omelet

Serves 1

COST: $0.78

Per omelet
Calories: 402
Fat: 31g
Carbohydrates: 4g
Protein: 25g
Fiber: 0g
Sugar: 1.5g
Sodium: 927mg

3 large eggs
¼ cup milk
¼ teaspoon salt
Dash of hot pepper sauce

1 teaspoon unsalted butter
2 tablespoons Boursin
1 teaspoon chopped chives

1. Whisk together the eggs, milk, salt, and hot pepper sauce. Melt the butter in an 8-inch nonstick skillet over medium-low heat (this is a case where a truly nonstick skillet is really important). Swirl the pan to thoroughly coat it with butter.
2. Add the egg mixture and allow the eggs to sizzle for a minute without disturbing them. Then, using a wooden implement or heatproof rubber spatula, scramble the still liquid-y eggs around in the pan; smooth out the top with your implement, and allow to cook, undisturbed, until the eggs are 90 percent set but still glistening on top (residual heat will cook the egg the rest of the way when you fold it).
3. Crumble the cheese into the center of the omelet. Fold the omelet in half, slide onto the plate, sprinkle with chives, and enjoy.

Cheese and Mushroom Frittata

Serves 4

COST: $1.67

Per ¼ frittata
Calories: 264
Fat: 23g
Carbohydrates: 5g
Protein: 10g
Fiber: 1g
Sugar: 3g
Sodium: 156mg

4 tablespoons olive oil, divided
6 large mushrooms, sliced
  (about 1¼ cups)
¼ cup chopped onion
3 large eggs
½ cup milk

⅛ teaspoon nutmeg
Salt and fresh-cracked pepper,
  to taste
1 small tomato, chopped
½ cup grated Cheddar cheese
4 slices French bread, toasted

1. Heat 2 tablespoons olive oil in a frying pan over medium-low heat. Add the mushrooms and onion. Cook until the onion is tender. Remove from pan and set aside. Clean the pan.
2. Lightly beat the eggs with the milk. Stir in the nutmeg, salt, and pepper. Stir in the cooked mushrooms and onion, the tomato, and ¼ cup grated cheese.
3. Heat the remaining 2 tablespoons olive oil in the frying pan on medium-low heat. Swirl the oil around the pan to coat the pan entirely. Pour the egg mixture into the pan. Move the vegetables around if necessary to make sure they are evenly mixed throughout the egg. Cook the frittata over medium-low heat. Tilt the pan occasionally or lift edges of the frittata with a spatula so that the uncooked egg runs underneath.
4. When the frittata is firm on top, cover the frying pan with a lid or plate. Turn the pan over so that the frittata falls onto the lid. Return the pan to the stovetop and slide the frittata back into the pan, so that the bottom of the frittata is on top. Sprinkle the remaining ¼ cup grated cheese over the frittata. Cook over medium-low heat until the cheese is melted and the frittata is cooked through. To serve, cut the frittata pizza-style into wedges and serve on top of the toasted French bread.

ⓥ Potato Poblano Breakfast Burritos

Serves 3

COST: $1.96

Per burrito
Calories: 265
Fat: 11g
Carbohydrates: 35g
Protein: 5g
Fiber: 5g
Sugar: 3g
Sodium: 453mg

2 tablespoons olive oil
2 small potatoes, diced small
2 poblano chilies, diced
1 teaspoon chili powder

Salt and pepper to taste
1 tomato, diced
3 flour tortillas, warmed

1. Heat olive oil in a pan and add potatoes and chilies, sautéing until potatoes are almost soft, about 6–7 minutes.
2. Add chili powder, salt and pepper, and tomato, and stir well to combine.
3. Continue cooking until potatoes and tomatoes are soft, another 4–5 minutes.
4. Warm the flour tortillas in the microwave for 10 seconds.
5. Wrap the potato mixture in the warm tortillas.

ⓥ Maple Cinnamon Breakfast Quinoa

Serves 4

COST: $0.85

Per 1 cup
Calories: 257
Fat: 4g
Carbohydrates: 48g
Protein: 8g
Fiber: 5g
Sugar: 13g
Sodium: 28mg

1 cup quinoa
2–2½ cups water
1 teaspoon coconut oil
⅔ cup soy milk

½ teaspoon cinnamon
2 tablespoons maple syrup
2 bananas, sliced

1. Heat the quinoa and water in a small saucepan and bring to a boil. Reduce to a simmer and allow to cook, covered, for 15 minutes, until liquid is absorbed.
2. Remove from heat and fluff the quinoa with a fork. Cover, and allow to sit for 5 minutes.
3. Stir in the coconut oil and soy milk, then add the remaining ingredients.

Scrambled Egg Burritos

Serves 4

1 tablespoon unsalted butter
1 medium onion, finely
   chopped (about 1 cup)
½ cup sliced roasted peppers
8 extra-large eggs, beaten
½ cup half-and-half

Few dashes of hot pepper
   sauce
1 cup shredded jalapeño jack
   cheese
Salt and pepper to taste
4 6-inch flour tortillas
Salsa

1. In a large skillet over medium heat, melt the butter; add the onions and sliced roasted peppers. Cook until the onions are soft and translucent, about 5 minutes. Combine the eggs and the half-and-half, and add them to the pan. Cook, stirring constantly with a wooden spoon, until the eggs are about half cooked—(still very runny); add the hot pepper sauce, cheese, salt, and pepper. Remove from heat. Eggs should be soft, creamy, and have small curds.

2. Soften the tortillas by placing them directly atop the stove burner on medium heat or putting them in the microwave for 10 seconds. Spoon ¼ of the egg mixture slightly off center on a tortilla. Fold the sides in upon the egg and roll the tortilla away from yourself, folding the filling in and tucking with your fingers to keep even pressure. Repeat with remaining tortillas. Serve with salsa.

ⓥ Tropical Breakfast Couscous

Serves 2

COST: $1.15

Per 2 cups
Calories: 289
Fat: 2g
Carbohydrates: 60g
Protein: 8g
Fiber: 5.5g
Sugar: 19g
Sodium: 29mg

1 cup couscous
1 cup coconut milk
1 cup orange juice

½ teaspoon vanilla
2 tablespoons honey
4 cups sliced fresh fruit

1. Prepare couscous per instructions listed on the box.
2. In a small saucepan, heat coconut milk and juice until just about to simmer. Do not boil.
3. Add couscous and heat for 1 minute. Stir in vanilla, cover, and turn off heat. Allow to sit, covered, for 5 minutes, until couscous is cooked.
4. Fluff couscous with a fork and stir in honey. Garnish with fresh fruit.

ⓥ Chocolate Peanut Butter Breakfast Quinoa

Serves 1

COST: $0.85

Per 1 cup
Calories: 359
Fat: 14g
Carbohydrates: 45g
Protein: 16g
Fiber: 6g
Sugar: 11g
Sodium: 142mg

½ cup quinoa
1½ cups almond milk
2 tablespoons peanut butter
1½ tablespoons cocoa

1½ tablespoons brown-rice syrup

1. Combine the quinoa and almond milk over medium-low heat. Cover and cook for 15 minutes or until quinoa is done, stirring frequently.
2. While still hot, stir in peanut butter, cocoa, and brown rice syrup.

Cinnamon Toast with Ricotta and Raisin Spread

Serves 1

COST: $0.51

Per 1 slice
Calories: 180
Fat: 4.5g
Carbohydrates: 30g
Protein: 7g
Fiber: 4g
Sugar: 8g
Sodium: 240mg

⅛ teaspoon (or to taste) ground cinnamon
2 teaspoons orange marmalade
3 tablespoons ricotta cheese
2 teaspoons (or to taste) raisins
1 slice bread

1. Preheat oven to 180°F. Spray a baking sheet with cooking spray.
2. In a small bowl, mash the ground cinnamon and marmalade into the ricotta cheese. Stir in the raisins. When thoroughly mixed, spread over the bread.
3. Place the bread on the prepared baking sheet. Bake for 15 minutes. Increase temperature to 200°F and bake for 5 more minutes. Serve warm.

French Toast

Serves 1

COST: $0.68

Per recipe
Calories: 284
Fat: 18g
Carbohydrates: 20g
Protein: 11g
Fiber: 3g
Sugar: 3g
Sodium: 292mg

2 eggs
Salt, to taste
¼ cup milk
2 tablespoons butter
2 slices sprouted grain bread
1 cup blueberries
¼ teaspoon cinnamon

1. In a small bowl, lightly beat the eggs. Add the salt and milk.
2. Heat the butter in a frying pan over medium-low heat.
3. Take a slice of bread and dip one side into the beaten egg, letting it sit for a few seconds to soak up the egg mixture. Turn the bread over and repeat with the other side.
4. Lay the bread flat in the frying pan. Repeat with the other slice of bread. Cook until the bread is browned on the bottom, then turn over and repeat with the other side.
5. Remove from the frying pan, top with berries, and sprinkle with cinnamon.

Serves 4

COST: $0.98

Per 2 slices
Calories: 271
Fat: 2g
Carbohydrates: 55g
Protein: 9g
Fiber: 3.5g
Sugar: 3g
Sodium: 494mg

2 bananas
½ cup almond milk
1 tablespoon orange juice
1 tablespoon maple syrup
¾ teaspoon vanilla

1 tablespoon flour
1 teaspoon cinnamon
½ teaspoon nutmeg
Coconut oil for frying
8 thick slices bread

1. Using a blender or mixer, mix together the bananas, almond milk, orange juice, maple syrup, and vanilla until smooth and creamy.
2. Whisk in flour, cinnamon, and nutmeg, and pour into a pie plate or shallow pan. Heat 1–2 tablespoons of coconut oil in a large skillet.
3. Dip or spoon mixture over each bread slice on both sides, and fry in hot oil until lightly golden brown on both sides, about 2–3 minutes.

The Perfect Vegan French Toast

Creating an eggless French toast is a true art. Is your French toast too soggy or too dry? Thickly sliced bread lightly toasted will be more absorbent. Too mushy or the mixture doesn't want to stick? Try spooning it onto your bread, rather than dipping.

Easy Pancake Roll-Ups

6 small pancakes

COST: $0.43

Per 2 pancakes
Calories: 414
Fat: 19g
Carbohydrates: 48g
Protein: 13g
Fiber: 2g
Sugar: 14g
Sodium: 556mg

2 teaspoons baking powder
⅛ teaspoon salt
1 cup buckwheat flour
2 tablespoons granulated
   sugar
1 egg

1½ tablespoons vegetable oil,
   plus extra for greasing
1 cup milk
6 tablespoons peanut butter
3 small bananas

1. Heat a griddle or heavy skillet, making sure it is very hot (a drop of water should sizzle when dropped on it).
2. In a medium-sized bowl, stir the baking powder and salt into the buckwheat flour, blending thoroughly. Stir in the sugar. In a small bowl, lightly beat the egg and add the vegetable oil and milk.
3. Add the egg mixture to the dry ingredients. Do not overmix. (Don't worry about lumps.) The batter should be runny.
4. Grease the griddle or skillet with oil as needed. Pour the batter into the pan in ½-cup portions for each pancake (or ¼-cup portions for smaller pancakes). Cook until the pancakes are browned on the bottom and bubbling on top. Flip over and cook the other side until browned. Remove the pancakes from the skillet or griddle.
5. Spread the peanut butter on the pancakes and roll up. Place banana slices inside pancake before rolling up.

How to Freeze Pancakes

This recipe is great for 3 meals if you freeze it, which will benefit you during that busy finals week. For best results, cool the cooked pancakes before freezing. Don't stack them during cooling, as the heat won't escape from the pancakes in the middle of the stack. Once the pancakes have cooled, stack them by placing a layer of wax paper between each pancake. Place the stacked pancakes in the freezer. Once they are frozen, remove the pile of pancakes, place them in a resealable plastic bag, and return to the freezer. Frozen pancakes will keep for 1–2 months.

Buckwheat Pancakes

Yields 12 pancakes

COST: $0.36

Per pancake
Calories: 90
Fat: 3g
Carbohydrates: 13g
Protein: 2g
Fiber: 2g
Sugar: 3g
Sodium: 240mg

¾ cup all-purpose flour
¼ cup buckwheat flour
2 teaspoons baking powder
1 teaspoon baking soda
⅛ teaspoon salt
3 tablespoons raw sugar

1 egg
1½ tablespoons coconut oil,
   plus extra for greasing
1 cup buttermilk
¾ cup frozen blueberries
1 tablespoon sesame seeds

1. Heat a griddle or heavy skillet, making sure it is very hot (water should sizzle when dropped on it).
2. In a medium-sized bowl, mix together the all-purpose and buckwheat flour. Stir the baking powder, baking soda, and salt into the flour, blending thoroughly. Stir in the sugar. In a small bowl, lightly beat the egg and add the coconut oil and buttermilk.
3. Add the egg and milk mixture to the dry ingredients. Do not overmix. (Don't worry about lumps.) The batter should be runny. Gently stir in the blueberries.
4. Grease the griddle or skillet with oil as needed. Pour the batter into the pan in 2-tablespoon portions. Sprinkle about ¼ teaspoon of sesame seeds on top of each pancake.
5. Cook until the pancakes are browned on the bottom and bubbling on top, about 3–5 minutes. Flip over and cook the other side until browned. Remove the pancakes from the skillet or griddle. Repeat with the remaining pancake batter. Serve.

Corny Polenta Breakfast Pancakes

Serves 8

COST: $0.34

Per 2 pancakes
Calories: 220
Fat: 5g
Carbohydrates: 37g
Protein: 5g
Fiber: 1g
Sugar: 7g
Sodium: 294mg

1 cup coarse yellow cornmeal
2 cups boiling water
1¼ cups flour
½ teaspoon table salt
2½ tablespoons sugar
4½ tablespoons baking powder

¾ cup milk
2 eggs plus 1 egg white, beaten
5 ounces (1¼ sticks) melted butter
1 cup blueberries
2 tablespoons maple syrup

1. Make the polenta by whisking the cornmeal directly into the boiling water. It should quickly thicken to a paste. Transfer immediately to a platter or pan to cool.
2. Sift together flour, salt, sugar, and baking powder. In a separate bowl, whisk together milk, eggs, and melted butter. Whisk flour mixture into egg mixture, mixing only as much as is necessary to combine. Crumble the cooled polenta into the batter, breaking up large pieces between your fingers. Adjust consistency of the batter with additional milk, if necessary, to achieve the consistency of thick oatmeal.
3. Cook on a hot buttered griddle, cast-iron skillet, or nonstick pan, forming 3- or 4-inch pancakes, cooking thoroughly on both sides. Serve with pure maple syrup and 1 cup of fruit.

Cottage Cheese Blintzes

Serves 4

COST: $1.62

Per blintze
Calories: 320
Fat: 14g
Carbohydrates: 33g
Protein: 13g
Fiber: 2g
Sugar: 13g
Sodium: 324mg

1 cup cottage cheese
½ cup ricotta
2 tablespoons sugar
1 large egg yolk

4 small whole grain tortillas
2 tablespoons unsalted butter, melted
4 tablespoons jam

1. Preheat oven to 325°F. In a food processor, pulse the cottage cheese, ricotta, and sugar until smooth. Transfer to a bowl; whisk in the yolk.
2. Butter a 9" × 13" baking dish. On a clean work surface, spoon a generous tablespoon of cheese filling onto the bottom third of a tortilla. Fold in the sides, and fold the bottom up to envelop the filling; roll the tortilla away from yourself. Repeat with remaining tortillas; line them into the baking dish and brush them with the melted butter. Bake 10–15 minutes, until they have become visibly plump. Serve with jam on the side.

Healthy Honey Banana Crepes

Yields 16 small or 8 regular crepes

COST: $2.68
Per 1 crepe
Calories: 179
Fat: 5g
Carbohydrates: 29g
Protein: 6.5g
Fiber: 3g
Sugar: 12g
Sodium: 218mg

2½ tablespoons honey
2 teaspoons baking powder
⅛ teaspoon salt
1 cup whole-wheat flour
3 eggs
1 cup buttermilk

1 cup water
1½ tablespoons coconut oil, or
  as needed
2 tablespoons toasted wheat
  germ

1. Melt the honey in a small saucepan over low heat.
2. In a medium-sized bowl, stir the baking powder and salt into the flour, blending thoroughly. In a small bowl, beat the eggs with the buttermilk, water, 1 tablespoon coconut oil, and melted honey.
3. Make a well in the middle of the dry ingredients and add the egg mixture. Stir until smooth. (If you have a blender or food processor, blend all the ingredients at medium speed.) Let the batter rest for at least 1 hour.
4. In a heavy skillet over medium heat, warm just enough vegetable oil to coat the bottom of the pan. Pour ¼ cup batter into the skillet. Rotate the pan so that the batter flows toward the edges and covers the bottom of the entire pan. Cook until browned on the bottom, turn over, and cook on the other side. Sprinkle with the toasted wheat germ. Repeat with the remaining batter.

Basic Waffle Recipe

Yields 6 waffles

COST: $0.23
Per waffle
Calories: 191
Fat: 9g
Carbohydrates: 22g
Protein: 13g
Fiber: 1g
Sugar: 6g
Sodium: 197mg

1 egg, separated
¼ cup melted butter
¾ cup plus 2 tablespoons milk
1½ teaspoons baking powder
⅛ teaspoon salt

2 tablespoons granulated
  sugar
½ teaspoon ground cinnamon
1 cup all-purpose flour

1. Preheat waffle iron. In a small bowl, use an electric mixer to beat the egg white until stiff. In another bowl, beat the egg yolk well and mix in the melted butter and milk.
2. In a medium-sized bowl, stir the baking powder, salt, sugar, and cinnamon into the flour, blending thoroughly.
3. Make a well in the middle of the flour mixture. Pour the beaten egg mixture into the well and stir into the dry ingredients. The batter should resemble a muffin batter. Gently fold in the egg white.
4. Cook the waffles according to the instructions on the waffle iron.

Oatmeal with a Twist

Serves 2

COST: $0.86
Per 1½ cups
Calories: 240
Fat: 12g
Carbohydrates: 26g
Protein: 8g
Fiber: 3g
Sugar: 9g
Sodium: 34mg

1 cup water
½ cup rolled oats (not the
  quick-cooking type)
3 teaspoons apple juice
3 tablespoons ricotta cheese

2 tablespoons raisins
¼ cup walnuts
1 teaspoon raw sugar
Ground cinnamon, to taste

1. Bring the water to a boil. Stir in the oats. Cover, reduce heat to low, and let the oats simmer for 10–15 minutes or until the water is nearly evaporated.
2. While the oats are cooking, stir the apple juice into the ricotta cheese, and then stir in the raisins.
3. Transfer the porridge to a large serving bowl. Stir in the ricotta cheese mixture, walnuts, and the sugar. Sprinkle with cinnamon, if desired. Serve hot with 1 cup of fruit for a complete breakfast.

Hawaiian Waffles with Macadamia Nuts

Yields 6 waffles

COST: $3.72

Per 2 waffles
Calories: 360
Fat: 20g
Carbohydrates: 39g
Protein: 7g
Fiber: 3g
Sugar: 8g
Sodium: 340mg

1 egg, separated
¼ cup melted butter
¾ cup plus 2 tablespoons buttermilk
1½ teaspoons baking powder
⅛ teaspoon salt

2½ tablespoons brown sugar
1 cup all-purpose flour
¼ cup chopped macadamia nuts
½ cup pineapple chunks, canned

1. Preheat waffle iron.
2. In a small bowl, use an electric mixer to beat the egg white until it is stiff. In a separate bowl, beat the egg yolk well and mix in the melted butter and buttermilk.
3. In a medium-sized bowl, stir the baking powder, salt, and brown sugar into the flour, blending thoroughly.
4. Make a well in the middle of the flour mixture. Pour the beaten egg mixture into the well and stir into the dry ingredients. The batter should resemble a muffin batter.
5. Gently fold in the egg white. Gently stir in the macadamia nuts and pineapple.
6. Cook the waffles according to the instructions on the waffle iron.

Waffle FAQ

The waffle's distinctive honeycombed shape immediately sets it apart from a pancake. However, differences between them can also be found in the batter. Waffle batters are normally high in butter, removing any need to grease a waffle pan before cooking. Egg whites make the batter light and fluffy.

Fresh Fruit Granola

Serves 2

COST: $1.55

Per 1 cup
Calories: 480
Fat: 16g
Carbohydrates: 69g
Protein: 12g
Fiber: 10g
Sugar: 31g
Sodium: 42mg

1 apple
½ cup dried dates
1 cup granola

½ cup milk
1 tablespoon honey

Chop the apple and dried dates. Combine the fruit with the granola in a bowl and pour the milk over the top. Drizzle the honey over the granola and fruit.

Ⓥ Vanilla Flax Granola

Yields 2½ cups

COST: $0.47

Per ¼ cup
Calories: 173
Fat: 6g
Carbohydrates: 26g
Protein: 4g
Fiber: 3g
Sugar: 6g
Sodium: 5mg

⅓ cup maple syrup
⅓ cup coconut oil
1½ teaspoons vanilla

2 cups oats
½ cup flax meal
¾ cup dried fruit, small dice

1. Preheat oven to 325°F.
2. Melt and whisk together maple syrup, coconut oil, and vanilla over low heat until margarine is melted.
3. Toss together oats, flax meal, and dried fruit on a large baking tray in a single layer (you may need to use two trays).
4. Drizzle maple syrup mixture over oats and fruit, gently tossing to combine as needed.
5. Bake for 25–30 minutes, carefully tossing once during cooking. Granola will harden as it cools.

Yogurt Surprise

Serves 1

COST: $1.03
Per 1½ cups
Calories: 327
Fat: 8g
Carbohydrates: 41g
Protein: 15g
Fiber: 4g
Sugar: 18g
Sodium: 129mg

¼ cup Cinnamon and Raisin Granola (see recipe in this chapter)

¾ cup vanilla yogurt
¼ small banana, sliced

Place 2 tablespoons granola in the bottom of a tall glass. Add 3 tablespoons yogurt. Continue layering by alternating even portions of the granola and yogurt. Top with the banana slices and serve.

Ⓥ Rosemary Tempeh Hash

Serves 4

COST: $1.29
Per ¾ cup
Calories: 207
Fat: 8g
Carbohydrates: 22g
Protein: 11g
Fiber: 3g
Sugar: 1.5g
Sodium: 10mg

2 potatoes, diced
1 8-ounce package tempeh, cubed
2 tablespoons olive oil

2 green onions, chopped
1 teaspoon chili powder
1 teaspoon rosemary
Salt and pepper to taste

1. Cover the potatoes with water in a large pot and bring to a boil. Cook just until potatoes are almost soft, about 15 minutes. Drain.
2. In a large pan, sauté the potatoes and tempeh in olive oil for 3–4 minutes, lightly browning tempeh on all sides.
3. Add green onions, chili powder, and rosemary, stirring to combine, and heat for 3–4 more minutes. Season well with salt and pepper.

Banana Muffins

Yields 12–15 muffins

COST: $0.22

Per muffin
Calories: 150
Fat: 5g
Carbohydrates: 22g
Protein: 3g
Fiber: 2g
Sugar: 5g
Sodium: 150mg

1 egg
1 cup milk
¼ cup vegetable oil
¾ teaspoon baking soda
¾ teaspoon baking powder
⅛ teaspoon salt

1½ cups all-purpose flour
3 tablespoons honey
1 cup mashed banana (about 2 bananas)
¼ teaspoon ground cinnamon

1. Preheat oven to 375°F. Grease a muffin pan.
2. In a small bowl, add the egg to the milk and beat lightly. Add the vegetable oil and stir to combine.
3. In a large bowl, combine the baking soda, baking powder, salt and flour, and stir until well blended.
4. Add the egg mixture to the flour mixture and stir to form a batter. Stir in the honey, banana, and ground cinnamon. Stir until combined but do not beat.
5. Spoon the batter into the muffin tins so that they are about ⅔ full. Bake for 20–25 minutes or until a toothpick inserted into the middle of a muffin comes out clean. Let cool for 5 minutes before serving. Store the muffins in a sealed tin.

Freezing Muffins

Got extra muffins? To freeze, wrap tightly in aluminum foil or place in a resealable plastic bag. To reheat, microwave briefly on high heat or warm in a 300°F oven for 15–20 minutes.

Blueberry Muffins

Yields about 12 muffins

COST: $0.30

Per muffin
Calories: 130
Fat: 4.5g
Carbohydrates: 21g
Protein: 3g
Fiber: 3g
Sugar: 8g
Sodium: 140mg

1 egg
1 cup buttermilk
3 tablespoons vegetable oil
¾ cup all-purpose flour
¾ cup whole-wheat flour
¼ cup oat bran

¾ teaspoon baking powder
½ teaspoon baking soda
⅛ teaspoon salt
⅓ cup brown sugar
1 cup blueberries, frozen

1. Preheat oven to 375°F. Grease a muffin pan.
2. In a small bowl, add the egg to the buttermilk and beat lightly. Add the vegetable oil and stir to combine.
3. In a large bowl, combine the all-purpose flour, whole-wheat flour, and oat bran. Stir in the baking powder, baking soda, salt, and brown sugar until well blended.
4. Add the egg mixture to the flour mixture and stir to form a batter. Be careful not to overmix the batter; don't worry if there are still lumps. Gently stir in the blueberries.
5. Spoon the batter into the muffin tins so that they are between ½ and ⅔ full. Bake for 20–25 minutes or until a toothpick inserted into the middle of a muffin comes out clean. Let cool for 5 minutes before eating. Store the muffins in a sealed tin.

Apple and Cinnamon Muffins

Yields 12 muffins

COST: $0.25
Per muffin
Calories: 160
Fat: 5g
Carbohydrates: 25g
Protein: 3g
Fiber: 3g
Sugar: 10g
Sodium: 140mg

1 egg
1 teaspoon vanilla extract
1 cup buttermilk
¼ cup vegetable oil
1½ teaspoons baking powder
½ teaspoon baking soda

Pinch salt
½ cup granulated sugar
1¾ cups all-purpose flour
¾ teaspoon ground cinnamon
½ teaspoon ground nutmeg
1½ cups diced apple

1. Preheat oven to 375°F. Grease a muffin pan. In a small bowl, add the egg and vanilla extract to the buttermilk and beat lightly. Add the vegetable oil and mix to combine.
2. In a large bowl, combine the baking powder, baking soda, salt, sugar, and flour and stir to blend well. Stir in the cinnamon and nutmeg. Add the egg mixture to the flour mixture and stir to form a batter. Be careful not to overmix the batter; don't worry if there are still lumps. Stir in the diced apples.
3. Spoon the batter into the prepared muffin tins so that they are between ½ and ⅔ full. Bake for 20 minutes or until a toothpick inserted into the middle of a muffin comes out clean. Let cool for 5 minutes before serving. Store the muffins in a sealed tin.

Ⓥ Carob Peanut Butter Banana Smoothie

Serves 2

COST: $1.31
Per ½ of recipe or 16 oz.
Calories: 254
Fat: 10g
Carbohydrates: 37g
Protein: 9g
Fiber: 7g
Sugar: 19g
Sodium: 119mg

7 or 8 ice cubes
2 bananas
2 tablespoons natural peanut
    butter

2 tablespoons carob powder
1 cup almond milk

Blend together all ingredients until smooth.

Marvelous Mango Muffins

Yields about 15 muffins

1¾ cups mango, diced
1 egg
¼ cup vegetable oil
1 cup sour cream
1½ teaspoons baking powder
⅛ teaspoon salt

1 cup granulated sugar
1½ cups all-purpose flour
½ teaspoon ground allspice
4 tablespoons water
¼ cup unsweetened coconut
flakes

1. Preheat oven to 375°F. Grease a muffin pan. Mash the mango into a soft pulp. In a small bowl, beat together the egg, vegetable oil, and sour cream. Combine thoroughly.
2. In a large bowl, combine the baking powder, salt, sugar, and flour, and stir until well blended. Stir in the ground allspice.
3. Add the egg mixture to the flour mixture and stir to form a batter. Be careful not to overmix the batter; don't worry if there are still lumps. Stir in the water. Stir in the mango and the coconut flakes.
4. Spoon the batter into the prepared muffin tins so that they are between ½ and ⅔ full. Bake for 25 minutes or until a toothpick inserted into the middle of a muffin comes out clean. Let cool for 5 minutes before serving. Store the muffins in a sealed tin.

It's All in the Baking Powder

Muffins get their distinctive domed shape from the addition of baking powder. When baking powder comes into contact with wet ingredients, carbon dioxide gas is released. This causes the batter to expand. The reaction is quick, so it's important to get muffins in the oven as quickly as possible after making the batter. Otherwise, too much gas escapes before they're heated, leading to flat-topped muffins.

Ⓥ Morning Cereal Bars

Yields 14 bars

COST: $0.52

Per bar
Calories: 285
Fat: 13g
Carbohydrates: 35g
Protein: 9g
Fiber: 4g
Sugar: 15g
Sodium: 137mg

3 cups whole grain flake breakfast cereal
1 cup natural peanut butter
⅓ cup tahini
1 cup maple syrup

½ teaspoon vanilla
2 cups muesli
½ cup flax meal
½ cup diced dried fruit

1. Lightly grease a baking pan or two casserole pans.
2. Place cereal in a sealable bag and crush partially with a rolling pin. If you're using a smaller cereal, you can skip this step. Set aside.
3. Combine peanut butter, tahini, and maple syrup in a large saucepan over low heat, stirring well to combine.
4. Remove from heat and stir in the vanilla, and then the cereal, muesli, flax meal, and dried fruit.
5. Press firmly into greased baking pan and chill until firm, about 45 minutes, then slice into bars.

Cinnamon and Raisin Granola

Yields about 3 cups

COST: $0.39

Per ½ cup
Calories: 285
Fat: 8g
Carbohydrates: 45g
Protein: 5g
Fiber: 4g
Sugar: 20g
Sodium: 6mg

2 cups rolled oats
2½ tablespoons toasted wheat
   germ
1 teaspoon ground cinnamon
6 tablespoons apple juice

2 tablespoons canola oil
1 tablespoon unsalted butter
2 tablespoons brown sugar
1 cup raisins

1. Preheat oven to 250°F.
2. In a large bowl, mix together the rolled oats and wheat germ. Stir in the ground cinnamon, apple juice, canola oil, and butter, blending thoroughly.
3. Spread the mixture on a baking sheet. Bake for 15 minutes, stirring regularly. Remove from the oven.
4. Pour the granola back into the mixing bowl. Stir in the brown sugar and raisins. Spread the mixture back onto the baking sheet. Cook for another 15–20 minutes or until the granola is golden brown. Let cool. Store in a sealed container.

Ⓥ Strawberry Protein Smoothie

Serves 2

COST: $0.83

Per ½ of recipe or 16 oz.
Calories: 148
Fat: 2g
Carbohydrates: 30g
Protein: 7g
Fiber: 3g
Sugar: 18g
Sodium: 6mg

½ cup frozen strawberries
½ block silken tofu
1 banana

¾ cup orange juice
3 or 4 ice cubes
1 tablespoon honey

Blend together all ingredients until smooth and creamy.

Protein Shakes

If you're tempted by those rows of fancy-looking dairy- and egg-based protein powders sold at your gym, try a vegan version! Well-stocked natural-foods stores sell a variety of naturally vegan protein powders that you can add to a smoothie for all your muscle-building needs. Look for hemp protein powder or flax-meal blends, and don't be afraid of the green proteins—some of them are quite tasty!

CHAPTER 2

Lunches

It is easy to skip lunch when you're rushing from class to class and just don't have the time to head back to your dorm or the cafeteria. However, if you go too long without eating—and anything more than 3 or 4 hours is really too long—your blood sugars and energy levels will crash, causing cravings for quick sources of energy throughout the rest of the day and night. This can lead to overeating . . . and to the gain of the unfortunate "freshman fifteen." The good news is that, with recipes like the Quinoa and Hummus Sandwich Wrap or the Simple Stuffed Pita Sandwich, you can bring your lunch with you if you're on the go. Or, with recipes like the Baked Tortilla Wraps or the Grilled Cheese Sandwich, you can take the time to create something delicious at home if you're lucky enough to have the afternoon free. So take the time to eat a healthy lunch. You'll be glad you did!

Bruschetta with Tomatoes

Serves 2

COST: $1.00

Per 2 slices
Calories: 257
Fat: 8g
Carbohydrates: 39g
Protein: 8g
Fiber: 2g
Sugar: 3g
Sodium: 419mg

1 clove garlic
1 medium tomato
Salt and pepper, to taste
4 slices French bread

1 tablespoon extra-virgin olive oil
½ teaspoon dried basil

1. Smash the garlic clove, peel, and cut in half. Wash the tomato and chop. Sprinkle the chopped tomato with salt and pepper and set aside.
2. Toast the bread slices. Rub the garlic over one side of each toasted bread slice.
3. Spread the chopped tomato on top. Drizzle with the olive oil. Sprinkle with the dried basil, if using, and add a bit of salt and pepper if desired.

Hearty Mexican Taco Salad

Serves 2

COST: $1.84

Per ½ salad or 2 cups
Calories: 261
Fat: 19g
Carbohydrates: 8g
Protein: 15g
Fiber: 2g
Sugar: 4g
Sodium: 507mg

2 lettuce leaves
½ red bell pepper
½ green bell pepper
1 small tomato

1 cup grated cheese mozzarella
3 tablespoons (or to taste) salsa
Taco chips

1. Wash and dry the vegetables.
2. Shred the lettuce leaves.
3. Seed the red and green peppers and chop.
4. Chop the tomato.
5. Combine the vegetables and grated cheese in a small salad bowl. Stir in the salsa. Serve with the taco chips.

Easy Falafel Patties

Serves 4

COST: $0.54

Per patty
Calories: 181
Fat: 2g
Carbohydrates: 32g
Protein: 9g
Fiber: 8g
Sugar: 5g
Sodium: 453mg

1 15-ounce can chickpeas, well drained
½ onion, minced
1 tablespoon flour
1 teaspoon cumin
¾ teaspoon garlic powder

¾ teaspoon salt
1 egg
¼ cup chopped fresh parsley
2 tablespoons chopped fresh cilantro

1. Preheat oven to 375°F.
2. Place chickpeas in a large bowl and mash with a fork until coarsely mashed. Or pulse in a food processor until chopped.
3. Combine chickpeas with onion, flour, cumin, garlic powder, salt, and egg, mashing together to combine. Add parsley and cilantro.
4. Shape mixture into 2-inch balls or 1-inch-thick patties and bake in oven for 15 minutes, or until crisp. Falafel can also be fried in oil for about 5–6 minutes on each side.

Falafel Sandwiches

Stuff falafel into a pita bread with some sliced tomatoes and lettuce and top it off with a bit of tahini, vegan tzatziki, or hummus for a Middle Eastern sandwich.

Black and Green Veggie Burritos

Serves 4

COST: $1.64

Per 1 burrito
Calories: 369
Fat: 10g
Carbohydrates: 52g
Protein: 11g
Fiber: 9g
Sugar: 8g
Sodium: 501mg

1 onion, chopped
2 zucchini, cut into thin strips
1 green bell pepper, chopped
2 tablespoons olive oil
½ teaspoon oregano
½ teaspoon cumin

1 15-ounce can black beans, drained
1 4-ounce can green chilies
1 cup cooked rice
4 large flour tortillas, warmed

1. Heat onion, zucchini, and bell pepper in olive oil until vegetables are soft, about 4–5 minutes.
2. Reduce heat to low and add oregano, cumin, black beans, and chilies, combining well. Cook, stirring, until well combined and heated through.
3. Place ¼ cup rice in the center of each flour tortilla and top with the bean mixture.
4. Fold the bottom of the tortilla up, then snugly wrap one side, then the other. Serve as is, or bake in a 350°F oven for 15 minutes for a crispy burrito.

Gluten-Free Bean Burritos

If you're gluten-free or just want an extra protein and nutrition boost, use a cooked grain other than rice in these burritos and shop for a gluten-free flatbread to wrap it up in. Quinoa in particular works well in burritos, as it is lighter than other grains.

Tempeh Dill "Chicken" Salad

Serves 3

COST: $1.15

Per ¾ cup
Calories: 237
Fat: 10g
Carbohydrates: 14g
Protein: 15g
Fiber: 2g
Sugar: 2g
Sodium: 237mg

1 8-ounce package tempeh, diced small
Water for boiling
3 tablespoons vegan mayonnaise
2 teaspoons lemon juice
½ teaspoon garlic powder
1 teaspoon Dijon mustard
2 tablespoons sweet pickle relish
½ cup green peas
2 stalks celery, diced small
1 tablespoon chopped fresh dill

1. Cover tempeh with water and simmer for 10 minutes, until tempeh is soft. Drain and allow to cool completely.
2. Whisk together mayonnaise, lemon juice, garlic powder, mustard, and relish.
3. Combine tempeh, mayonnaise mixture, peas, celery, and dill and gently toss to combine.
4. Chill for at least 1 hour before serving to allow flavors to combine.

Curried Chicken Tempeh

For curried chicken salad, omit the dill and add ½ teaspoon curry powder and a dash of cayenne and black pepper. If you don't feel up to dicing and simmering tempeh, try combining the dressing with store-bought mock chicken, or even veggie turkey or deli slices.

Greek Salad Pita Pockets

Serves 1

COST: $2.30

Per 1 pita pocket
Calories: 320
Fat: 12g
Carbohydrates: 41g
Protein: 12g
Fiber: 3g
Sugar: 1g
Sodium: 837mg

1 pita pocket
½ tomato
2 romaine lettuce leaves
8 cucumber slices
¼ cup crumbled feta cheese

6 whole olives, chopped
2 tablespoons extra-virgin
olive oil
Salt and freshly cracked black
pepper, to taste

1. Cut the pita pocket in half. Cut the tomato into thin wedges. Shred the romaine lettuce leaves.
2. In a medium-sized bowl, toss the lettuce and tomato with the cucumber.
3. Add the feta cheese, chopped olives, and olive oil, and toss again. Sprinkle with the salt and freshly cracked black pepper.
4. Fill each pita half with half of the salad, and serve.

Quinoa and Hummus Sandwich Wrap

Serves 1

COST: $2.47

Per 1 wrap
Calories: 332
Fat: 10g
Carbohydrates: 38g
Protein: 11g
Fiber: 8g
Sugar: 2g
Sodium: 364mg

1 tortilla, warmed
3 tablespoons hummus
⅓ cup cooked quinoa
½ teaspoon lemon juice

2 teaspoons vinaigrette salad
dressing
1 roasted red pepper, sliced
into strips
¼ cup sprouts

Spread a warmed tortilla or wrap with a layer of hummus, then quinoa, and drizzle with lemon juice and salad dressing. Layer red pepper and sprouts on top, and wrap.

Asian Lettuce Wrap Sandwich

Serves 2

COST: $2.69
Per sandwich
Calories: 435
Fat: 18g
Carbohydrates: 48g
Protein: 24g
Fiber: 10g
Sugar: 7g
Sodium: 360mg

2 teaspoons rice vinegar
2 teaspoons soy sauce
1 teaspoon raw honey
1 teaspoon cornstarch
2 teaspoons water
6 ounces tempeh
3 tablespoons vegetable oil, or as needed
1 clove garlic, smashed and peeled
3 tablespoons chopped onion
⅓ cup chopped red bell pepper
¼ cup bean sprouts
3 drops sesame seed oil, or to taste
1 romaine lettuce leaf, shredded
4 tortilla wraps

1. In a small bowl, combine the rice vinegar, soy sauce, and honey, and set aside.
2. Mix the cornstarch and water; set aside in a separate small bowl. Chop the tempeh into bite-sized pieces.
3. Add 2 tablespoons vegetable oil to a frying pan and heat on medium-high heat. When the oil is hot, add the garlic. Fry briefly, using a spatula to move the garlic through the oil. Add the tempeh and stir-fry until cooked on all sides, stirring constantly, about 7 minutes. Remove from the pan and set aside.
4. Add 1 or 2 more tablespoons vegetable oil to the pan. Add the onion and stir-fry for about 1 minute. Add the red pepper and stir-fry for another minute. Add the bean sprouts.
5. Add the rice vinegar mixture to the pan, pouring it in the middle of the vegetables. Give the cornstarch and water mixture a quick restir. Turn the heat up to medium high and add the cornstarch mixture. Cook, stirring constantly, until it boils and thickens. Add the tempeh and mix with the vegetables and sauce. Sprinkle the sesame seed oil over the top.
6. Place a few pieces of shredded lettuce on each wrap, spoon ¼ of the tempeh and sauce mixture over the top of each, and roll up. If using pita pocket halves, place the shredded lettuce and ¼ of the tempeh mixture inside each half. If using a tortilla wrap, roll it up.

Bell Pepper Types

Ever wonder what the difference is between green, orange, and red bell peppers? Actually, all three come from the same plant. The main difference is that red and orange bell peppers have been allowed to ripen longer on the vine. The extra ripening time gives red bell peppers a sweeter flavor than green bell peppers, making them a popular salad ingredient.

Black Bean and Barley Taco Salad

Serves 2

COST: $1.99

Per ½ of recipe or
  3 cups
Calories: 343
Fat: 3g
Carbohydrates: 68g
Protein: 18g
Fiber: 19g
Sugar: 12g
Sodium: 860mg

1 15-ounce can black beans,
  drained
½ teaspoon cumin
½ teaspoon oregano
2 tablespoons lime juice
1 teaspoon hot chili sauce
1 cup cooked barley

1 head iceberg lettuce,
  shredded
¾ cup salsa
Handful tortilla chips,
  crumbled
2 tablespoons vegan Italian
  dressing

1. Mash together the beans, cumin, oregano, lime juice, and hot sauce until beans are mostly mashed, then combine with barley.
2. Layer lettuce with beans and barley and top with salsa and tortilla chips. Drizzle with Italian dressing. Serve.

Make It Well-Rounded

Lunch is a great opportunity to utilize plant proteins, like beans, nuts, whole grains, and soy proteins. They contain vitamins, minerals, and fiber to help you increase your energy levels throughout your day. You will get the most out of your lunch by choosing a protein, whole grain, and at least 1 or 2 cups of vegetables.

Serves 2

COST: $1.29
Per 1 wrap
Calories: 293
Fat: 17g
Carbohydrates: 22g
Protein: 16g
Fiber: 4g
Sugar: 2g
Sodium: 93mg

4 ounces tempeh
1 teaspoon olive oil
3 tablespoons chopped red onion
¼ small green bell pepper, finely chopped
1 tablespoon red wine vinegar
2 soft tortilla wraps
2 tablespoons natural peanut butter

1. Preheat oven to 350°F. Spray a baking sheet with cooking spray.
2. Cut the tempeh into thin strips. Heat the olive oil in a frying pan over medium heat. Add the onion and cook until tender. Add the green pepper and cook for 1–2 minutes.
3. Push the vegetables off to the side of the pan and add the tempeh in the middle, laying the strips out flat. Splash the red wine vinegar over the tempeh. Cook until the tempeh is browned on both sides, turning over once. Mix the vegetables in with the tempeh and vinegar. Remove from heat and let cool briefly.
4. Lay 1 tortilla wrap flat on a plate and spread peanut butter on the inside. Add half the tempeh and vegetable mixture on the bottom of the wrap, making sure the filling isn't too close to the edges. Fold in the right and left sides of the wrap. Roll up and tuck in the edges. Repeat with the other tortilla wrap.
5. Place both wraps on the prepared baking sheet. Bake for 15 minutes or until heated through.

Flatbread FAQ

Many cuisines have a special type of flatbread, from Middle Eastern pita to Indian naan and Mexican tortillas. Despite their flat shape, some flatbreads contain a leavener (an ingredient to make the dough or batter rise). Double-layered breads (such as pita) may use either sourdough or yeast as a leavener, while single-layered Italian focaccia is always made with yeast.

Grilled Cheese Sandwich

Serves 1

COST: $1.87

Per 1 sandwich
Calories: 519
Fat: 31g
Carbohydrates: 37g
Protein: 22g
Fiber: 3g
Sugar: 2g
Sodium: 590mg

2 tablespoons softened butter
2 slices bread

2 teaspoons (or to taste) mustard
2 slices Cheddar cheese

1. Spread about 1½ teaspoons butter over one side of a slice of bread. Spread the mustard over one side of the other slice. Place the cheese slices in the middle and close the sandwich, dry sides out.
2. Heat a frying pan over medium heat for about 1 minute. When the frying pan is hot, melt 1 table-spoon of butter in the frying pan (it should be sizzling).
3. Add the sandwich to the frying pan. Cook until the bottom is golden brown, 3–4 minutes. Press down gently on the sandwich with a spatula while it is cooking.
4. Push the sandwich to the side and add about 2 teaspoons of butter to the pan. Turn the sand-wich over and cook on the other side until browned and the cheese is nearly melted, 3–4 min-utes. Remove the sandwich from the pan and cut in half.

Sprouted-Grain Bread?

A better choice than white bread, sprouted-grain bread is more digestible, richer in protein, and higher in vitamins and minerals. It is made from wheat berries that are allowed to sprout and that are then ground coarsely. However, they are not ground into a flour like most other bread flours, which is why this bread is often thought to be "flourless." It does contain gluten and often contains a variety of grains and legumes, such as lentil, millet, barley, and oat.

Egg Salad Sandwich

Serves 2

COST: $1.07

Per sandwich
Calories: 230
Fat: 10g
Carbohydrates: 21g
Protein: 13g
Fiber: 3g
Sugar: 3g
Sodium: 410mg

2 Hard-Boiled Eggs (see Chapter 1)
1 tablespoon whole plain Greek yogurt
2 teaspoons Dijon mustard

⅛ teaspoon (or to taste) paprika
Salt and pepper, to taste
1 lettuce leaf
¼ small tomato
2 pita pocket halves

1. Peel the eggs, chop, and place in a small bowl. Mash the eggs with the Greek yogurt and the Dijon mustard. Stir in the paprika, salt, and pepper.
2. Shred the lettuce leaf. Finely chop the tomato to yield about 2 heaping tablespoons. Stir the lettuce and tomato into the egg mixture.
3. If using bread, spread half of the mixture on 1 slice of bread. Place the other slice on top and close. If using pita pockets, stuff half of the egg mixture into each pocket. If not eating immediately, store in a resealable plastic bag or a plastic container in the refrigerator until ready to eat.

Wheat and Corn Wraps with Tofu

Serves 4

COST: $1.88

Per 1 wrap
Calories: 321
Fat: 11g
Carbohydrates: 50g
Protein: 8g
Fiber: 4g
Sugar: 4g
Sodium: 269mg

½ cup wheat berries, boiled until tender, usually about 30 minutes
1 package (10 ounces) frozen sweet corn, thawed
Juice of 1 lemon
1 tablespoon extra-virgin olive oil

½ teaspoon ground cumin
Salt and pepper to taste
2 tablespoons salad dressing
4 medium flour tortillas
1 cup store-bought flavored tofu

1. In a bowl, toss the cooked grain, corn, lemon juice, olive oil, cumin, salt, and pepper until combined.
2. Spread the dressing in a line across the equator of each tortilla. Spoon in the grain salad; arrange the tofu alongside the grain, and roll the tortilla up.

Serves 4

COST: $0.74

Per 1 burger
Calories: 202
Fat: 4g
Carbohydrates: 32g
Protein: 8g
Fiber: 2g
Sugar: 2g
Sodium: 33mg

3 ounces firm tofu
3 tablespoons quick-cooking oats
1 tablespoon finely chopped onion
1 tablespoon Worcestershire sauce
Dash (or to taste) chili powder

1 egg
1 teaspoon olive oil
½ cup crushed tomatoes
1 tablespoon (or to taste) white vinegar
1 teaspoon (or to taste) granulated sugar
4 English muffins

1. Drain the tofu and crumble. Stir in the oats, onion, Worcestershire sauce, and chili powder. Add the egg and mix together with your hands to make sure the tofu is thoroughly mixed with the other ingredients.
2. Heat the olive oil in a frying pan. Form the tofu mixture into balls approximately the size of large golf balls and flatten with the palm of your hand. Add the burgers to the frying pan, using a spatula to gently flatten them and push together any portions that are separating from the main burger. Cook the burgers for 3–4 minutes on each side, until browned.
3. Heat the crushed tomatoes, vinegar, and sugar in a small saucepan. Taste and adjust the seasoning if desired. Keep warm on low heat while toasting the English muffins.
4. Split the muffins in half and toast. Serve open-faced, with a portion of the tomato mixture spooned onto one muffin half and the burger on the other.

Ⓥ Eggless Egg Salad

Serves 4

COST: $0.78

Per ¾ cup
Calories: 290
Fat: 24g
Carbohydrates: 10g
Protein: 10g
Fiber: 2g
Sugar: 2g
Sodium: 428mg

1 block firm tofu
1 block silken tofu
½ cup vegan mayonnaise
⅓ cup sweet pickle relish
¾ teaspoon apple cider vinegar

½ stalk celery, diced
2 tablespoons minced onion
1½ tablespoons Dijon mustard
2 tablespoons chopped chives
1 teaspoon paprika

1. In a medium-sized bowl, use a fork to mash the tofu together with the rest of the ingredients, except the paprika.
2. Chill for at least 15 minutes before serving to allow flavors to mingle. Garnish with paprika just before serving.

Simple Stuffed Pita Sandwich

Serves 2

COST: $1.24

Per ½ pita
Calories: 248
Fat: 11g
Carbohydrates: 25g
Protein: 11g
Fiber: 2g
Sugar: 6g
Sodium: 290mg

½ small firm, crisp, hardy apple
½ celery stalk
1 leaf romaine lettuce
2 Cheddar cheese slices

3 teaspoons low-calorie Caesar dressing
1 tablespoon chopped walnuts
1 pita pocket

1. Wash and dry the apple, celery, and lettuce. Cut the celery into thin slices. Core the apple and chop finely. Shred the lettuce. Cut the cheese first horizontally and then vertically into tiny pieces.
2. Mix together the apple, celery, lettuce, cheese, salad dressing, and chopped walnuts. Refrigerate in a sealed container for at least 2 hours to give the flavors a chance to combine.
3. Cut the pita in half. Stuff half the filling into each pita half.

Ⓥ Avocado-Beet Wraps with Succotash

Serves 4

COST: $2.75

Per 1 filled wrap
Calories: 321
Fat: 14g
Carbohydrates: 38g
Protein: 13g
Fiber: 8.5g
Sugar: 4g
Sodium: 225mg

4 flour tortillas (10-inch diameter)
2 tablespoons vegan mayonnaise
2 cups Succotash Salad (see Chapter 4)

1 large or 2 small beets (about 8 ounces), boiled until tender, peeled
1 ripe Florida avocado, peeled and cut into 1-inch wedges
Kosher salt

1. Soften the tortillas by placing them directly into the microwave on a plate for 10–20 seconds.
2. Spread ½ tablespoon mayonnaise into a line across the center of each tortilla. Spoon ½ cup succotash onto each tortilla. Halve the beets, and cut the halves into ½-inch slices. Divide the beets and avocado slices evenly onto the tortillas, placing them on the side of the succotash line closest to you. Sprinkle with salt.
3. Place 1 of the tortillas on a work surface directly in front of yourself. Fold the near edge of the tortilla over the fillings, and roll it, jellyroll fashion, away from yourself, keeping even pressure to ensure a tight roll. Place seam-side down on a plate; repeat with remaining tortillas.

Fiber Intake

Fiber is the most important part of each meal because it helps regulate blood sugars, energy levels, fullness, weight, and heart health, and it promotes a healthy digestive system. It is recommended to consume 25–38 grams of fiber per day. Sources should stem from vegetables, fruit, and whole grains.

Serves 4

COST: $2.81

Per 2 slices
Calories: 355
Fat: 15g
Carbohydrates: 46g
Protein: 10g
Fiber: 5g
Sugar: 7g
Sodium: 473mg

¼ cup extra-virgin olive oil
¼ cup balsamic vinegar
1 tablespoon Dijon mustard
½ bunch fresh oregano,
   roughly chopped
½ bunch Italian parsley,
   roughly chopped
1 small bunch chives, chopped

2 ripe beefsteak tomatoes,
   sliced ½-inch thick
2 yellow acid-free tomatoes,
   sliced ½-inch thick
8 slices Branola or other type
   sweet-dough bread contain-
   ing whole grains, ½-inch thick
Coarse salt and black pepper
   to taste

1. Whisk together oil, vinegar, and mustard in a small steel bowl. Fold in chopped herbs.
2. Lay tomato slices in a single layer into a glass (nonreactive) dish, and pour most of the dressing over them, reserving about 2 tablespoons. Allow to marinate at room temperature for about 10 minutes.
3. Toast the whole-grain bread and drizzle with remaining dressing. Shingle tomatoes in alternating colors. Season with coarse salt and freshly ground black pepper.

Ⓥ Middle Eastern Hummus

Serves 4

COST: $1.94

Per 3 pita wedges
Calories: 368
Fat: 8g
Carbohydrates: 59g
Protein: 16g
Fiber: 11g
Sugar: 7g
Sodium: 182mg

2 large cloves garlic
1 19-ounce can chickpeas
4 tablespoons reserved juice
   from chickpeas
2 tablespoons, plus 1 teaspoon
   lemon juice

2 tablespoons tahini
¼ teaspoon (or to taste) ground
   cumin
2 pita pockets (4 pita halves)

1. Preheat oven to 350°F. Smash, peel, and finely chop the garlic cloves. Drain the chickpeas and mash them, reserving the juice from the can.
2. In a small bowl, blend together the chopped garlic, mashed chickpeas, chickpea juice, lemon juice, tahini, and cumin to create homemade hummus.
3. Cut 2 pita pockets into 6 wedges each. Place on a baking sheet and toast in the oven for 8–10 minutes, until crispy. Spread a heaping tablespoon of hummus on each pita wedge. Store the remainder of the hummus in a sealed container in the refrigerator until ready to use.

Replacing Tahini with Peanut Butter

Peanut butter makes a handy (and less expensive) alternative to tahini in recipes. Both lend a creamy texture and nutty flavor to dishes such as Middle Eastern Hummus. However, tahini is the winner in the nutrition department. While their fat and calorie content are nearly identical, tahini is loaded with vitamins and minerals such as calcium and lecithin.

Portobello Mushroom Burger

Serves 1

COST: $3.03

Per ½ English muffin
Calories: 332
Fat: 17g
Carbohydrates: 34g
Protein: 10g
Fiber: 4g
Sugar: 4g
Sodium: 303mg

1 English muffin, cut in half
2 teaspoons butter
1 large portobello mushroom
1 romaine lettuce leaf
1 teaspoon olive oil

3 tablespoons (or to taste) chopped onion
1 tomato slice
2 tablespoons grated Swiss cheese

1. Toast the English muffin halves. Spread 1 teaspoon butter on both halves while still warm, and set aside. Wipe the portobello mushroom with a damp cloth and cut into thin slices. Wash the lettuce leaf, dry, and tear into pieces.
2. Heat the olive oil on medium in a skillet. Add the chopped onion and cook on medium-low heat until tender.
3. Add the remaining 1 teaspoon butter to the frying pan. Push the onion to the side and lay the portobello mushroom slices flat in the pan. Cook until browned on the bottom, about 2 minutes. Turn over and cook the other side until browned. Add the tomato slice to the pan while the mushroom is cooking for the last 2 minutes.
4. When the mushroom slices are browned on both sides, sprinkle the grated cheese on top. Cook briefly until the cheese is melted.
5. To make the burger, lay the tomato on 1 muffin half and place the cooked onion on the other half. Lay the mushroom and melted cheese mixture on top of both halves. Serve open-faced, garnished with the lettuce.

Portobello Pita with Buckwheat and Beans

Serves 4

COST: $3.50

Per pita pocket
Calories: 311
Fat: 10g
Carbohydrates: 47g
Protein: 9g
Fiber: 4g
Sugar: 3g
Sodium: 370mg

4 medium-sized portobello mushrooms, stems removed
Kosher salt and freshly ground black pepper
1 tablespoon olive oil
4 pita pocket breads, medium size (about 8 inches)

2 tablespoons mayonnaise
1 cup buckwheat groats, cooked according to directions on package
¼ pound cooked green beans

1. Brush the portobello caps clean (do not wash under water); season with salt and pepper. Heat oil in a large skillet until very hot, but not quite smoking. Cook the mushrooms top-side down over high heat until cooked through, about 4 minutes. Small pools of juice should appear where the stem was removed.

2. Cut an opening in a pita; slather the inside with mayonnaise. Spoon in a layer of cooked buckwheat groats (or kasha), and add ¼ of the green beans. Stuff in 1 mushroom cap. Repeat with remaining pitas.

Pesto Pizza

Serves 2

COST: $1.51

Per ½ pizza
Calories: 247
Fat: 14g
Carbohydrates: 20g
Protein: 12g
Fiber: 3g
Sugar: 2g
Sodium: 460mg

4 mushrooms
3 tablespoons jarred basil and tomato pesto sauce

1 pita pocket
⅓ cup grated mozzarella cheese

1. Wipe the mushrooms clean with a damp cloth and slice.
2. Spread the pesto sauce on the pita pocket. Lay the mushroom slices on the sauce. Sprinkle the cheese on top.
3. Place the pita pocket on a microwave-safe plate or a paper towel. Microwave on high heat for 3–5 minutes, until the cheese melts.

Split English Muffins with Mornay Sauce

Serves 4

COST: $1.48

Per 1 English muffin
Calories: 237
Fat: 8g
Carbohydrates: 31g
Protein: 8g
Fiber: 2g
Sugar: 2g
Sodium: 312mg

4 English muffins
4 poached eggs (see Basic Poached Egg earlier in this chapter)
1½ tablespoons butter
1½ tablespoons all-purpose flour

¾ cup milk
¼ cup shredded Parmesan cheese
1 teaspoon prepared mustard
¼ teaspoon ground nutmeg
Salt and pepper, to taste

1. Split the English muffins in half and toast.
2. Melt the butter in a small saucepan over low heat. Stir in the flour. Cook on low heat for 3 minutes, stirring continually. Gradually whisk in the milk. Whisk in the cheese. Stir in the prepared mustard, nutmeg, and salt and pepper.
3. Place 1 cooked egg on one half of an English muffin. Spoon ¼ of the sauce on the other half and close up the muffin. Repeat with the remaining muffins.

Stuffed Potato

Serves 1

1 large (about 8 ounces) baking potato
1 tablespoon Greek yogurt
½ tablespoon butter
¼ teaspoon paprika
⅛ teaspoon salt
Pepper, to taste
2 teaspoons shredded Cheddar cheese

1. Wash the potato, scrubbing off any dirt. Pierce the potato in several spots with a fork.
2. Place the potato on a paper plate or microwave-safe plate and microwave on high heat for 3–7 minutes, until cooked through. Let the potato sit for about 1 minute before removing from the microwave.
3. Slice the potato open. Carefully scoop out most of the potato, leaving about ¼ inch pulp around the skin. Mash the potato pulp with the yogurt, butter, paprika, salt, and pepper. Sprinkle the shredded cheese on top.
4. Spoon the mixture into the potato shell and microwave for 3–5 minutes, until the cheese melts.

Potato Cooking Times

The time it takes to cook a potato in the microwave can vary quite a bit, depending on the size of the potato and the strength of your microwave. To be safe, cook the potato on high heat for 3 minutes, check it with a fork, and then continue cooking in 2-minute segments as required. The potato is cooked when it is tender and can easily be pierced with a fork. The skin may also be slightly wrinkled.

CHAPTER 3

Snacks, Dips, and Spreads

Snacking has a purpose; you should use snacks to bridge the gap between your meals and keep your metabolism working in peak form. You know that you are going to be hungry, so plan for it. Instead of running on the fly to make impulse buys at the vending machine, make a plan to have healthy and easy-to-carry foods readily available for your snacks like the Chewy Granola Bars, Spiced Pecans, and Popcorn Munchies found in this chapter. It's well worth the effort to make sure you have something on hand as strategic snacking can help keep you stay focused and be more productive—which is especially important whether you're going up against a big exam or getting ready to ace an important presentation. The challenge is to make the best choice at the time and not give in to temptation to eat something unhealthy. Snack healthy!

Breadsticks with Cheese

Serves 2

COST: $1.50

Per ½ of recipe
Calories: 194
Fat: 4g
Carbohydrates: 32g
Protein: 8g
Fiber: 2g
Sugar: 2.5g
Sodium: 535mg

½ tomato
4 tablespoons vegan cream
  cheese
2 tablespoons milk

½ teaspoon dried parsley
  flakes
12 whole-grain pretzel sticks

Chop the tomato finely. Mix together the cheese, chopped tomato, milk, and parsley flakes to make a dip for the breadsticks. Serve as is, or purée the cheese in the blender for a smoother dip.

Supreme Pizza Crackers

Serves 2

COST: $1.30

Per 3 pizza wedges
Calories: 178
Fat: 7.5g
Carbohydrates: 19g
Protein: 8.5g
Fiber: 2g
Sugar: 2g
Sodium: 272mg

3 tablespoons tomato sauce
1 pita pocket
2 large mushrooms, sliced

2 tablespoons sliced olives
⅓ cup grated Cheddar

Spread the tomato sauce on the pita pocket. Add the mushroom slices and the olives. Sprinkle the cheese over the top. Broil for about 2–3 minutes, until the cheese melts. Cut into 6 wedges.

Chewy Granola Bars

Yields about 16 bars

COST: $0.30
Per 1 bar
Calories: 185
Fat: 12g
Carbohydrates: 16g
Protein: 5g
Fiber: 2 g
Sugar: 7g
Sodium: 10mg

8 tablespoons coconut oil
¼ cup, plus 2 tablespoons honey
2 cups rolled oats
2 tablespoons toasted wheat germ

¾ teaspoon ground cinnamon
1 tablespoon sesame seeds
2 eggs
½ cup raisins
½ cup chopped peanuts

1. Preheat oven to 300°F.
2. Melt the coconut oil with the honey in a small saucepan on low heat, stirring continuously.
3. In a large bowl, combine the rolled oats, wheat germ, ground cinnamon, and sesame seeds. Add melted coconut oil and honey to the dry ingredients and stir to mix. Lightly beat the eggs and add them to the mixture, stirring to combine. Stir in the raisins and chopped peanuts.
4. Spread the mixture in a 9" × 9" pan, pressing it down with a spatula to spread it out evenly. Bake for 15 minutes or until golden brown. Let cool and cut into bars.

Crisp Potato Pancakes

Serves 4

COST: $2.37
Per 2 pancakes
Calories: 264
Fat: 2.5g
Carbohydrates: 54g
Protein: 8g
Fiber: 4g
Sugar: 3g
Sodium: 106mg

1 large egg
3 large baking potatoes (such as Idaho russet), peeled
1 medium onion

⅛ teaspoon sea salt
1 tablespoon flour (whole wheat)
Coconut oil for frying

1. Beat egg in a large bowl. Using the large-hole side of a box grater, shred the potatoes into the lengthiest shreds possible. Grate in the onion. Add the salt and sprinkle in the flour; toss with your hands to mix.
2. Heat the oil until it shimmers but does not smoke (potato should sizzle upon entry). Form 8 pancakes from the batter, and pan-fry them in batches of 3 or 4, squeezing out excess water before sliding them into the pan. Cook slowly, without moving them for the first 5 minutes; then loosen with a spatula. Turn after about 8 minutes, when the top appears ⅓ cooked. Finish cooking on other side, about 4 minutes more. Drain on paper towels.

Fricos (Cheese Crisps)

Serves 4

COST: $2.00

Per 4 crisps
Calories: 66
Fat: 5g
Carbohydrates: 0.5g
Protein: 5g
Fiber: 0g
Sugar: 0g
Sodium: 382mg

1 cup finely shredded
  Parmigiano-Reggiano

Heat a nonstick skillet over medium heat. Sprinkle 1 tablespoon cheese into a small mound in the pan. Cook until the bottom is nicely browned, then transfer to drain on paper towels. They are soft and oozy, and require a little practice to handle them properly, so have a little extra cheese ready in case the first few are "less than perfect."

Spinach and Artichoke Dip

Serves 12

COST: $1.01

Per ¼ cup
Calories: 90
Fat: 7g
Carbohydrates: 4g
Protein: 6g
Fiber: 2g
Sugar: 2g
Sodium: 118mg

2 15-ounce cans quartered
  artichoke hearts, drained
  and rinsed
1 red pepper, chopped finely
1 green pepper, chopped finely
1 10-ounce package frozen
  spinach

3 cloves garlic, minced
1 cup plain Greek yogurt
8 ounces cream cheese
White pepper
¼ cup Parmesan cheese

Preheat the oven to 325°F. Mix together all ingredients except Parmesan cheese. Spread into a 9" × 9" baking dish or 1½-quart casserole dish, sprinkle Parmesan over the top, and bake 30 minutes until golden brown. Serve with whole-grain crackers and raw vegetables.

Spicy White Bean–Citrus Dip

Serves 12

COST: $0.50

Per ⅓ cup
Calories: 70
Fat: 0.5g
Carbohydrates: 12g
Protein: 4g
Fiber: 4g
Sugar: 3g
Sodium: 257mg

2 15-ounce cans white navy beans, drained and rinsed
¼ cup plain Greek yogurt
Zest of 1 orange, grated
1 teaspoon chipotle purée
1 teaspoon lime juice
¼ teaspoon sea salt
½ cup diced white onions
1 tablespoon chopped cilantro

Purée the beans, Greek yogurt, orange zest, chipotle purée, lime juice, and salt in a food processor until smooth. Add onions and cilantro; mix with a rubber spatula until combined.

Parsley and Onion Dip

Serves 6

COST: $0.42

Per ¼ cup
Calories: 54
Fat: 3g
Carbohydrates: 4g
Protein: 5g
Fiber: 1g
Sugar: 2g
Sodium: 104mg

1 onion, chopped
3 cloves garlic, minced
1 tablespoon olive oil
1 block firm tofu, well pressed
½ teaspoon onion powder
3 teaspoons lemon juice
¼ cup chopped fresh parsley
2 tablespoons chopped fresh chives
¼ teaspoon salt

1. Sauté onions and garlic in oil for 3–4 minutes until onions are soft. Remove from heat and allow to cool slightly.
2. Process the onion and garlic with the tofu, onion powder, and lemon juice in a food processor or blender until onion is minced and tofu is almost smooth.
3. Mash together with remaining ingredients by hand.

Roasted Cashew and Spicy Basil Pesto

Serves 3

COST: $1.23

Per ¼ cup
Calories: 169
Fat: 8g
Carbohydrates: 12g
Protein: 17g
Fiber: 2.5g
Sugar: 1g
Sodium: 204mg

4 cloves garlic
1 cup Thai basil, packed
⅔ cup roasted cashews
½ cup nutritional yeast
¼ teaspoon salt

½ teaspoon black pepper
⅓ cup olive oil

Place all ingredients except the olive oil in blender or food processor and blend until smooth. Slowly incorporate olive oil until desired consistency is reached.

Traditional Pesto

For a more traditional Italian pesto, you can, of course, use regular Italian basil. In this case, cut back on the garlic a bit, and use pine nuts or walnuts instead of roasted cashews.

Salsa Fresca (Pico de Gallo)

Serves 8

COST: $1.14

Per ¼ cup
Calories: 15
Fat: 0g
Carbohydrates: 3.5g
Protein: 1g
Fiber: 1g
Sugar: 2g
Sodium: 141mg

4 medium tomatoes, seeded and diced fine (about 1½ cups)
1 small white onion, finely chopped

1 jalapeño pepper, seeded and finely chopped
½ teaspoon salt
2 teaspoons lime juice
¼ cup chopped cilantro

In a blender or food processor, purée one-third of the tomatoes. Combine with remaining tomatoes, onion, jalapeño, salt, lime juice, and cilantro. Best if used within 2 days. Serve with chips, with a cheese omelet, or as a sauce with other Mexican foods.

Ⓥ Vegan Chocolate Hazelnut Spread

Yields 1 cup

COST: $0.92

Per tablespoon
Calories: 148
Fat: 11g
Carbohydrates: 9g
Protein: 3g
Fiber: 3g
Sugar: 6g
Sodium: 1mg

2 cups hazelnuts, chopped
½ cup cocoa powder
½ cup powdered sugar

½ teaspoon vanilla
4 tablespoons vegetable oil

1. Add hazelnuts, cocoa powder, sugar, and vanilla to food processor, and process to combine.
2. Add oil, just a little bit at a time, until mixture is soft and creamy and desired consistency is reached. You may need to add a bit more or less than the 4 tablespoons.

Ⓥ Baba Ghanouj

Serves 4

COST: $1.12

Per ½ cup
Calories: 131
Fat: 9g
Carbohydrates: 12g
Protein: 3g
Fiber: 6g
Sugar: 4g
Sodium: 157mg

2 cloves garlic, peeled
1 whole eggplant, roasted 1
   hour in a 400°F oven, cooled,
   pulp scooped out
1 tablespoon tahini
¼ teaspoons kosher salt
2–3 teaspoons toasted cumin
   powder

Juice of 2 lemons
⅛ cup extra-virgin olive oil,
   plus a little extra for garnish
Freshly ground black pepper
Paprika for garnish
Parsley, to taste
Pita bread for dipping

1. In a food processor, chop the garlic until it sticks to the walls of the processor bowl. Add eggplant pulp, tahini, salt, cumin, and half of the lemon juice. Process until smooth, gradually drizzling in the olive oil. Season to taste with black pepper, additional salt, and lemon juice if necessary.
2. Spread onto plates, and garnish with a drizzle of extra-virgin olive oil, a few drops of lemon juice, a dusting of paprika, and some chopped parsley. Serve with wedges of warm pita bread.

No-Bake Tex-Mex Nachos

Serves 4

COST: $0.75

Per 8-oz. serving
Calories: 222
Fat: 11g
Carbohydrates: 23g
Protein: 7g
Fiber: 4.5g
Sugar: 2g
Sodium: 356mg

4½ ounces tortilla chips
1½ cups canned chili-style red
  kidney beans

2 teaspoons vegetable oil
2 tablespoons Greek yogurt
½ cup grated Cheddar cheese

1. Lay the tortilla chips on a baking sheet. Add more chips if necessary to cover the baking sheet.
2. Drain the kidney beans. Mash the beans by hand or purée in a food processor.
3. Heat the oil in a frying pan on medium. Add the mashed kidney beans and heat through, stirring. Stir in the yogurt.
4. Carefully spoon the kidney bean mixture onto the tortilla chips. Sprinkle with the grated cheese and serve.

Ⓥ Potato Pakoras (Fritters)

Serves 8

COST: $0.75

Per 1 fritter
Calories: 86
Fat: 2g
Carbohydrates: 12g
Protein: 4g
Fiber: 3g
Sugar: 2g
Sodium: 158mg

1¼ cups sifted chickpea flour
2 teaspoons coconut oil
1½ teaspoons ground cumin
½ teaspoon cayenne
¼ teaspoon turmeric
½ teaspoons salt

Approximately ½ cup cold
  water
Oil for frying
1 large or 2 medium baking
  potatoes (about 8 ounces),
  peeled, then sliced into
  ⅛-inch pieces

1. In a food processor or blender, pulse flour, oil, cumin, cayenne, turmeric, and salt 3 or 4 times until fluffy. With blade spinning, gradually add water, processing for 2–3 minutes until smooth. Adjust consistency by adding water until the mixture is slightly thicker than the consistency of heavy cream. Cover and set aside for 10 minutes.
2. Heat fry oil to 350°F. Dip potato slices into batter one by one, and slip them into the fry oil in batches of 6 or 7. Fry 4–5 minutes each side, until golden brown and cooked through. Serve immediately.

Ⓥ Vegan Cheese Ball

Makes 1 large cheese ball or 12 bite-sized cheese balls

COST: $0.48

Per 1 cheese ball
Calories: 130
Fat: 10g
Carbohydrates: 1g
Protein: 4g
Fiber: 1g
Sugar: 1g
Sodium: 158mg

1 block vegan nacho cheese, room temperature
1 container vegan cream cheese, room temperature
1 teaspoon garlic powder
½ teaspoon hot sauce
¼ teaspoon salt
1 teaspoon paprika
¼ cup nuts, finely chopped

1. Grate vegan cheese into a large bowl, or process in a food processor until finely minced. Using a large fork, mash the vegan cheese together with the cream cheese, garlic powder, hot sauce, and salt until well mixed. (You may need to use your hands for this.)
2. Chill until firm, at least 1 hour, then shape into ball or log shape, pressing firmly. Sprinkle with paprika and carefully roll in nuts. Serve with crackers.

Ⓥ Vegan Tzatziki

Yields 1½ cups

COST: $1.16

Per ½ cup
Calories: 75
Fat: 3g
Carbohydrates: 7g
Protein: 3g
Fiber: 1g
Sugar: 4g
Sodium: 10mg

1½ cups vegan soy yogurt, plain
1 tablespoon olive oil
1 tablespoon lemon juice
4 cloves garlic, minced
2 cucumbers, grated or chopped fine
1 tablespoon chopped fresh mint

Whisk together yogurt with olive oil and lemon juice until well combined. Combine with remaining ingredients. Chill for at least 1 hour before serving to allow flavors to mingle. Serve cold.

Spiced Pecans

Yields 3 cups

COST: $2.04

Per ½ cup
Calories: 209
Fat: 21g
Carbohydrates: 4g
Protein: 3g
Fiber: 3g
Sugar: 1.5g
Sodium: 128mg

1 ounce (2 tablespoons) unsalted butter
1 pound whole, shelled pecans

2 tablespoons light soy sauce
1 tablespoon hoisin sauce
A few drops hot pepper sauce

1. Preheat oven to 325°F. Melt butter in a large skillet. Add nuts; cook, tossing occasionally, until nuts are well coated. Add soy sauce, hoisin sauce, and hot pepper sauce; cook 1 minute more. Stir to coat thoroughly.
2. Spread nuts into a single layer on a baking sheet. Bake until all liquid is absorbed and nuts begin to brown. Remove from oven. Cool before serving.

Glazed Pecans

Yields 1 cup

COST: $2.09

Per ¼ cup
Calories: 257
Fat: 22g
Carbohydrates: 15g
Protein: 3g
Fiber: 3g
Sugar: 12g
Sodium: 2mg

2 tablespoons unsalted butter
⅛ cup brown sugar
1 tablespoon honey

1 teaspoon ground cinnamon
1 cup pecans

1. Melt the butter over low heat in a small saucepan. Add the brown sugar, honey, and ground cinnamon. Add the pecans, stirring to coat in the mixture.
2. Increase heat to medium and bring to a boil, stirring to dissolve the brown sugar.
3. Pour the pecan mixture onto a greased baking sheet and cool. Separate the mixture and store in an airtight container or plastic bag. (They will last for about 1 week.)

Spiced Nuts

Yields 4 cups

COST: $1.00
Per ½ cup
Calories: 266
Fat: 24g
Carbohydrates: 10g
Protein: 5g
Fiber: 2g
Sugar: 7g
Sodium: 1mg

2 cups walnut halves
4 tablespoons unsalted butter

4 tablespoons raw sugar
2 teaspoons five-spice powder

1. Preheat oven to 350°F.
2. Place the walnuts on an ungreased baking sheet. Toast for 8–10 minutes, checking frequently near the end of the baking time to make sure they do not burn.
3. While the nuts are toasting (about 2 or 3 minutes before they are finished), begin melting the butter on low heat in a frying pan. Add the sugar, stirring to dissolve. Stir in the five-spice powder.
4. Add the toasted nuts, and stir to coat. Cook briefly until the liquid is nearly absorbed. Pour the walnuts onto the ungreased baking sheet and separate. Let cool.

Caramel Walnuts

Yields 1 cup

COST: $0.97
Per ¼ cup
Calories: 266
Fat: 19g
Carbohydrates: 21g
Protein: 5g
Fiber: 2g
Sugar: 18g
Sodium: 9mg

¼ cup granulated sugar
1 tablespoon honey

2 tablespoons unsweetened
  condensed milk
1 cup walnut pieces

1. In a medium-sized saucepan, stir together the sugar, honey, and milk over low heat. Add the walnut pieces, stirring to make sure they are entirely coated in the sugar mixture. Increase heat to medium and bring to a boil. Let boil for several minutes, stirring occasionally, as the sugar darkens. When it has browned on the edges, remove from the heat.
2. Pour the walnut mixture onto a greased baking sheet and cool. Separate the walnuts and store in an airtight container or plastic bag. (They will last for about 1 week.)

ⓥ Avocado and Shiitake Pot Stickers

Yields 12 pot stickers

COST: $0.65

Per 3 dumplings
Calories: 83
Fat: 6g
Carbohydrates: 5g
Protein: 3g
Fiber: 3g
Sugar: 1g
Sodium: 65mg

1 avocado, diced small
½ cup shiitake mushrooms,
   diced
½ block silken tofu, crumbled
1 clove garlic, minced

2 teaspoons balsamic vinegar
1 teaspoon soy sauce
12 vegan dumpling wrappers
Water for steaming

1. In a small bowl, gently mash together all ingredients, except wrappers, just until mixed and crumbly.
2. Place about 1½ teaspoons of the filling in the middle of each wrapper. Fold in half and pinch closed, forming little pleats. You may want to dip your fingertips in water to help the dumplings stay sealed if needed.
3. To steam: Carefully place a layer of dumplings in a steamer, being sure the dumplings don't touch. Place steamer above boiling water and allow to cook, covered, for 3–4 minutes.

Whether Steamed or Fried . . .

In dumpling houses across East Asia, dumplings are served with a little bowl of freshly grated ginger, and diners create a simple dipping sauce from the various condiments on the table. To try it, pour some rice vinegar and a touch of soy sauce over a bit of ginger and add hot chili oil to taste.

Cheese Fondue

Serves 6

COST: $1.03 PER ⅙ RECIPE
Calories: 297
Fat: 20g
Carbohydrates: 9g
Protein: 19g
Fiber: 0g
Sugar: 5g
Sodium: 140mg

1 clove garlic
4 cups grated Swiss cheese
2 teaspoons cornstarch
¼ teaspoon (or to taste) nutmeg

1 cup apple juice
About 20 breadsticks

1. Cut the garlic clove in half. Rub it over the insides of a 2-quart microwave-safe casserole dish.
2. Add the cheese to the casserole dish and stir in the cornstarch and nutmeg. Add the apple juice and mix thoroughly.
3. Place the casserole dish in the microwave and microwave on high heat for 3 minutes. Stir, then microwave for 3 more minutes in 30-second intervals, stirring each time. Serve in a warmed fondue pot or in the casserole dish. (Serving in the casserole dish will make it easier to reheat if necessary.) Serve with the breadsticks for dipping.

Wild Mushroom Ragout in Puff Pastry Shells

Serves 8

COST: $0.29
Per 3 pieces
Calories: 56
Fat: 4g
Carbohydrates: 4g
Protein: 1g
Fiber: 0g
Sugar: 0g
Sodium: 165mg

24 pieces frozen puff pastry hors d'oeuvre shells
1 tablespoon unsalted butter
2 cups (about ½ pound) assorted wild mushrooms, such as morels, chanterelles, oysters, shiitakes, and/or domestic and cremini mushrooms
½ teaspoon salt

2 sprigs fresh rosemary, leaves picked and chopped
¼ cup vegetable stock
1 teaspoon cornstarch dissolved in 1 tablespoon cold water
Freshly ground black pepper to taste
Squeeze of lemon

1. Bake puff pastry shells according to package directions. In a medium skillet over medium heat, melt the butter. Add the mushrooms and cook without stirring for 5 minutes, until a nice brown coating has developed. Add salt and rosemary; cook 3 minutes more. Add the stock and cornstarch; stir until thickened and bubbling. Remove from heat; adjust seasoning with black pepper, a few drops of lemon juice, and salt to taste.
2. Spoon ½ teaspoon mushroom ragout into each shell. Serve piping hot.

Mini Goat Cheese Pizzas

Serves 8

COST: $1.13
Per 3 mini pizzas
Calories: 229
Fat: 7g
Carbohydrates: 33g
Protein: 7g
Fiber: 2g
Sugar: 1.5g
Sodium: 381mg

1 package frozen puff pastry dough (17 ounces; 2 sheets), thawed
½ cup marinara sauce
1 4-ounce package fresh goat cheese
1 tablespoon chopped fresh thyme

1. Preheat oven to 400°F. Using a 1-inch diameter cookie cutter, or the top of a small bottle, cut 24 disks of puff pastry; line onto an ungreased baking sheet. Stack another matching pan atop the disks, and bake until golden brown, about 15 minutes. The second pan will keep the disks from rising too high.
2. Make a slight indentation on each disk with the tip of a small knife. Spoon in a bit of marinara sauce, crumble on a pinch of goat cheese, and sprinkle with chopped thyme. To serve, warm again in the oven for 1 minute, until the goat cheese attains a slight shimmer; serve hot.

Ⓥ Walnut Asparagus "Egg" Rolls

Yields 15 egg rolls

COST: $1.24
Per 1 egg roll
Calories: 219
Fat: 10g
Carbohydrates: 31g
Protein: 5g
Fiber: 3g
Sugar: 1g
Sodium: 89mg

1 bunch asparagus
2 avocados, pitted
½ onion, minced
1 teaspoon lime juice
1 tablespoon soy sauce
1 teaspoon chipotle powder
½ cup walnuts, finely chopped
¼ cup chopped fresh cilantro
15 vegan egg roll wrappers
Oil for frying

1. Steam the asparagus until crisp-tender, then chop into ½-inch slices.
2. Mash together the asparagus with the avocados, onion, lime juice, soy sauce, chipotle powder, walnuts, and cilantro.
3. Place 2–3 tablespoons of filling in each wrapper. Fold the bottom up, then fold the sides in and roll, wetting the edges with water to help it stick together.
4. Fry in hot oil for 1–2 minutes on each side.

Tomato and Dill–Stuffed Grape Leaves (Dolmas)

Yields about 2 dozen dolmas

COST: $3.74

Per 4 stuffed leaves
Calories: 223
Fat: 9g
Carbohydrates: 31g
Protein: 4g
Fiber: 2g
Sugar: 1g
Sodium: 230mg

3 scallions, chopped
1 tomato, diced small
¼ cup olive oil, divided
1 cup uncooked rice
½ cup water
½ teaspoon salt
1 tablespoon chopped fresh dill

1 teaspoon dried parsley
1 tablespoon chopped fresh mint
40 grape leaves
Water for boiling
2 tablespoons lemon juice

1. Heat scallions and tomato in 2 tablespoons olive oil for 2 minutes, then add rice, water, salt, dill, parsley, and mint. Cover and cook for 5 minutes. Remove from heat and cool.
2. Place about 2 teaspoons of the rice filling in the center of a grape leaf near the stem. Fold the bottom of the leaf over the filling, then fold in the sides, and roll. Continue with each grape leaf.
3. Line the bottom of a pan with extra or torn grape leaves to prevent burning. Add wrapped and filled leaves, then add enough water just to cover the dolmas. Add remaining 2 tablespoons olive oil and bring to a slow simmer.
4. Cook for 20 minutes. Drizzle with lemon juice just before serving.

In a Hurry?

Mix together some leftover rice with vegan pesto for the filling. Wrap, simmer just a few minutes, and eat!

Granola Biscotti

Yields about 30 cookies

COST: $0.20

Per 1 cookie
Calories: 110
Fat: 2g
Carbohydrates: 20g
Protein: 3g
Fiber: 1g
Sugar: 9g
Sodium: 30mg

4 eggs
1 teaspoon vanilla extract
½ teaspoon almond extract
1½ cups all-purpose flour
1 cup rolled oats
½ teaspoon baking powder
⅛ teaspoon salt

1 tablespoon toasted wheat germ
½ cup brown sugar
½ cup granulated sugar
½ cup toasted almonds
½ cup chopped dates

1. Preheat oven to 325°F. Grease a large baking sheet.
2. In a small bowl, lightly beat the eggs with the vanilla and almond extracts. In a large bowl, combine the flour, rolled oats, baking powder, salt, toasted wheat germ, brown sugar, and granulated sugar. Blend thoroughly. Add the beaten eggs and blend to form a sticky dough. Stir in the toasted almonds and chopped dates.
3. Cut the dough in half. Flour your hands and shape each half into a 14-inch log. Place the logs on the prepared baking sheet and bake for 30 minutes or until a toothpick inserted into the center comes out clean. Let cool for 10 minutes.
4. Cut the dough diagonally into slices about ½-inch thick. Place the biscotti cut-side down on two ungreased baking sheets. Bake for a total of 15 minutes, removing the baking sheets from the oven at the halfway point and turning the biscotti over.
5. Return the biscotti to the oven, moving the baking sheet that was on the top rack to the bottom rack and vice versa (to ensure the cookies cook evenly). Let cool. Store the biscotti in a cookie tin or other airtight container.

Biscotti

An Italian creation, biscotti are oblong-shaped, crunchy biscuits that are perfect for dunking in tea or coffee. The secret to biscotti lies in baking the dough twice: first to cook it through, and then a second time to add extra crispness. (The word *biscotti* means "twice-baked" in Italian.)

Healthy Popcorn with Yogurt

Yields 1½ cups

COST: $0.87

Per recipe
Calories: 140
Fat: 2g
Carbohydrates: 30g
Protein: 4g
Fiber: 2g
Sugar: 19g
Sodium: 23mg

1½ cups popped popcorn
3 tablespoons plain yogurt

1 tablespoon liquid honey
¼ teaspoon nutmeg

Place the popcorn in a small bowl. Combine the yogurt and honey. Add to the popcorn, tossing to mix. Sprinkle with the nutmeg.

Popcorn Munchies

Yields 6 cups

COST: $0.98

Per 1 cup
Calories: 228
Fat: 11g
Carbohydrates: 30g
Protein: 3g
Fiber: 1.5g
Sugar: 11g
Sodium: 357mg

4 tablespoons butter
4 tablespoons condensed
  mushroom soup
¼ teaspoon dried parsley
  flakes

¼ teaspoon dried thyme
¼ teaspoon red pepper flakes
4 cups store-bought caramel
  popcorn
2 cups pretzel mix

1. In a frying pan, melt the butter over low heat. When it starts to melt, stir in the soup. Stir in the parsley, thyme, and red pepper flakes.
2. Place the popcorn in a medium-sized bowl. Pour the soup mixture over, stirring to make sure it is thoroughly mixed. Stir in the pretzel mix. Sprinkle extra red pepper flakes over, and serve.

Italian Pesto Popcorn

Yields 15 cups

COST: $1.25
Per 3 cups
Calories: 205
Fat: 13g
Carbohydrates: 18g
Protein: 4g
Fiber: 3.5g
Sugar: 0g
Sodium: 134mg

⅓ cup butter
1 teaspoon dried basil
¼ teaspoon garlic salt

2 teaspoons grated Parmesan cheese
15 cups popped popcorn

1. In a small saucepan, melt the butter over low heat. Stir in the basil, garlic salt, and Parmesan cheese.
2. Spread the popcorn out on a large tray. Slowly pour the melted butter mixture over the popcorn, stirring to make sure it is mixed thoroughly.

Baked Pita Chips with Yogurt Dressing

Serves 2

COST: $1.18
Per 6 dressed pita wedges
Calories: 205
Fat: 3g
Carbohydrates: 36g
Protein: 7.5g
Fiber: 2g
Sugar: 4g
Sodium: 498mg

2 pita pockets
Olive oil, as needed
½ cup plain yogurt
⅛ teaspoon (or to taste) garlic salt
1 teaspoon lemon juice

1 tablespoon chopped red onion
2 sprigs fresh parsley, finely chopped
Salt and pepper, to taste

1. Preheat oven to 350°F.
2. Cut the pitas in half, and cut each half into 3 wedges. Brush both sides of each wedge with the olive oil.
3. Place the pita wedges on a baking sheet and bake for 8–10 minutes, turning over once halfway through the cooking time.
4. Combine the yogurt, garlic salt, lemon juice, chopped red onion, and parsley. Season with salt and pepper. Spoon a heaping tablespoon of the mixture on each pita chip, or serve the dip on the side.

Homemade Trail Mix

Yields 1¾ cups

COST: $0.45

Per ⅓ cup
Calories: 250
Fat: 14g
Carbohydrates: 31g
Protein: 4g
Fiber: 3
Sugar: 8g
Sodium: 45mg

1 cup granola
¼ cup salted peanuts
¼ cup semisweet chocolate
  chips

¼ cup dehydrated banana
  chips
2 tablespoons hazelnuts

Combine all the ingredients in a medium-sized bowl. Pack in a resealable plastic bag or container for easy carrying. If not using immediately, store in an airtight container.

Fruit with Yogurt

Serves 2

COST: $2.05

Per 1 cup
Calories: 322
Fat: 21g
Carbohydrates: 28g
Protein: 8g
Fiber: 4g
Sugar: 22g
Sodium: 47mg

½ cup cherries
⅔ cup fruit cocktail, drained
¾ cup plain Greek yogurt

½ cup walnuts
¼ teaspoon ground cinnamon

Mix all the ingredients together in a large bowl. Cover the bowl with aluminum foil and freeze until solid.

Endive Spears with Herb Cheese

Serves 6

COST: $1.49

Per 2 spears
Calories: 110
Fat: 7g
Carbohydrates: 9g
Protein: 7g
Fiber: 1g
Sugar: 0g
Sodium: 460mg

12 Belgian endive spears
6 ounces flavored Boursin
  cheese

Chopped fresh parsley, for
  garnish

Fan the endive spears on a serving platter. Spread about 1 teaspoon (½ ounce) of the Boursin cheese at the base of each spear. Garnish with chopped parsley and serve.

Ⓥ Guacamole

Serves 8

COST: $0.62

Per ½ cup
Calories: 90
Fat: 7g
Carbohydrates: 6g
Protein: 1g
Fiber: 3g
Sugar: 1g
Sodium: 200mg

2 large, ripe avocados
1 medium-sized red tomato
1 small yellow onion
½ cup canned jalapeño
  peppers

1 tablespoon lime juice
½ teaspoon salt
½ teaspoon ground black
  pepper

1. Cut the avocados in half lengthwise and pry out the pits. Remove the peels and cut the avocados into 1-inch pieces. Mash with a fork.
2. Cut the tomato into ½-inch pieces. Remove the skin from the onion and cut into ¼-inch pieces. Drain off the liquid from the jalapeño peppers and cut the peppers into ¼-inch pieces.
3. Combine all the ingredients; mix well.

Marinated Artichoke Hearts

Serves 2

COST: $1.28
Per 2 dressed arti- choke hearts Calories: 170 Fat: 14g Carbohydrates: 10g Protein: 3g Fiber: 5g Sugar: 2g Sodium: 55mg

4 canned artichoke hearts
½ tomato
⅛ cup extra-virgin olive oil
1 tablespoon lemon juice

¼ teaspoon garlic powder
Salt and freshly cracked black
  pepper, to taste

1. Squeeze any excess juice from the canned artichokes. Wash the tomato, pat dry, and slice.
2. In a small bowl, combine the olive oil, lemon juice, garlic powder, and salt and pepper.
3. Pour the marinade into a resealable plastic bag. Add the artichokes and tomatoes and seal the bag. Refrigerate overnight to give the flavors a chance to blend.

Creamy Open Artichoke Sandwich

Serves 2

COST: $1.97
Per 1 sandwich Calories: 283 Fat: 12g Carbohydrates: 36g Protein: 8.5g Fiber: 6g Sugar: 3g Sodium: 537mg

½ recipe Marinated Artichoke
  Hearts (see recipe in this
  chapter)
¼ cup plain cream cheese

1 tablespoon chopped red
  onion
¼ teaspoon red pepper flakes
4 slices crusty rye bread

1. Chop the artichoke hearts and the tomato slices prepared from the Marinated Artichoke Hearts recipe. Stir in the cream cheese, chopped red onion, and red pepper flakes. Process in a food processor or blender until the mixture is smooth but still a bit chunky.
2. Spread approximately 2 heaping tablespoons of the cream cheese and artichoke mixture on each slice of bread. Broil for 3–5 minutes, until the spread is heated through. Store any leftover spread in a sealed container in the refrigerator.

V French Fries from Scratch

Serves 4

5 cups vegetable oil for frying,
  or more as needed
4 large baking potatoes

1. Add the oil to a deep-sided heavy saucepan or a wok. Heat the oil until it is at least 350°F.
2. While the oil is heating, wash and peel the potatoes. Cut lengthwise into pieces about ¼-inch thick. Place in a bowl of cold water for 5 minutes. Drain thoroughly and dry with paper towels.
3. Make sure paper towels are handy near the stove before you begin deep-frying. To cook, carefully slide the sliced potatoes into the hot oil, a handful at a time. Deep-fry for 4–5 minutes, until golden brown and crispy. Carefully remove with a slotted spoon and drain on paper towels. Fry the next batch.
4. When all the potatoes have been fried once, raise the oil temperature to 375°F. Deep-fry the French fries a second time for about 2 minutes, until crispy. Remove with a slotted spoon and drain. Serve with salt, ketchup, or vinegar as desired.

CHAPTER 4

Salads and Dressings

Some days—maybe after you splurged on pizza or heavy take-out food the night before—you just want to eat something light, and salads like the Apple and Walnut Salad and the Italian White Bean and Fresh Herb Salad, found in this chapter, are the perfect way to go. But what's a salad without dressing? Exactly! That's why you'll also find vegetarian recipes for favorites like Dairy-Free Ranch Dressing, Raspberry Vinaigrette, and Creamy Miso Sesame Dressing in this chapter as well. Enjoy!

Garden Salad

Serves 1

COST: $1.78

Per 1 salad
Calories: 108
Fat: 4g
Carbohydrates: 14g
Protein: 4g
Fiber: 5g
Sugar: 8g
Sodium: 382mg

4 iceberg lettuce leaves
½ tomato
2 celery stalks
½ cup sliced mushrooms
½ cup baby carrots

2 tablespoons low-calorie
  salad dressing

1. Wash the lettuce leaves, tomato, and celery stalks, and slice. Wipe the mushrooms with a damp cloth.
2. Chop the baby carrots in half. Combine the salad ingredients and toss with the salad dressing.

Vegetable-Cleaning Tip

Always wash fresh produce just before serving or eating, not when you first store the food in the crisper section of the refrigerator because produce will not spoil as quickly.

Rainbow Salad with Fennel

Serves 2

COST: $2.23
Per 2 cups
Calories: 190
Fat: 7g
Carbohydrates: 32g
Protein: 4g
Fiber: 7g
Sugar: 15g
Sodium: 260mg

1 carrot
1 red bell pepper
2 cups shredded red cabbage
2 tablespoons, plus 2 teaspoons vegan mayonnaise

3 teaspoons honey
1 fennel bulb

1. Wash the carrot and red pepper. Grate the carrot (there should be ½ to ⅔ cup grated carrot). Cut the red pepper into thin strips.
2. Mix together the carrot, red pepper, and cabbage in a bowl. Mix the mayonnaise with the honey. Toss the vegetables with the mayonnaise mixture.
3. Rinse the fennel under running water and pat dry. Trim off the top and bottom of the fennel bulb.
4. Cut the fennel into quarters, remove the core in the middle, and cut into thin slices. Garnish the salad with the fennel.

Simple Caesar Salad

Serves 3

COST: $0.76
Per 1 cup
Calories: 176
Fat: 10g
Carbohydrates: 13g
Protein: 7g
Fiber: 3g
Sugar: 4g
Sodium: 340mg

¾ head romaine lettuce
1 cup plain croutons
¼ cup grated Parmesan cheese

3 tablespoons Caesar salad dressing
Black pepper, to taste

1. Wash the lettuce and pat dry. Tear the leaves into strips approximately 1 inch wide.
2. Mix together the croutons, Parmesan cheese, and lettuce. Just before serving, toss with the Caesar salad dressing and sprinkle with black pepper.

V You Are a Goddess Dressing

Yields 1½ cups

⅔ cup tahini
¼ cup apple cider vinegar
⅓ cup soy sauce (low sodium)
2 teaspoons lemon juice

1 clove garlic
¾ teaspoon sugar
⅓ cup olive oil

1. Process all the ingredients, except olive oil, together in a blender or food processor until blended.
2. With the blender or food processor on high speed, slowly add in the olive oil, blending for another full minute, allowing the oil to emulsify.
3. Chill in the refrigerator for at least 10 minutes before serving; dressing will thicken as it chills.

In Search of Tahini

Tahini is a sesame seed paste native to Middle Eastern cuisine with a thinner consistency and milder flavor than peanut butter. You'll find a jarred or canned version in the ethnic foods aisle of large grocery stores, or a fresh version chilling next to the hummus if you're lucky.

Ⓥ Basic Balsamic Vinaigrette

Yields 1 cup

COST: $0.76

Per tablespoon
Calories: 63
Fat: 7g
Carbohydrates: 0g
Protein: 0g
Fiber: 0g
Sugar: 1g
Sodium: 50mg

¼ cup balsamic vinegar
½ cup olive oil
1 tablespoon Dijon mustard
¼ teaspoon salt

⅛ teaspoon black pepper
½ teaspoon dried basil
½ teaspoon dried parsley

Whisk together all ingredients with a fork until well combined.

Ⓥ Succotash Salad

Serves 8

COST: $0.59

Per ⅓ cup
Calories: 134
Fat: 7g
Carbohydrates: 16g
Protein: 3g
Fiber: 3g
Sugar: 1g
Sodium: 74mg

8 ears sweet corn, shucked (or 16 ounces top-quality frozen corn)
2 16-ounce cans red kidney beans, drained and rinsed

¼ cup rice wine vinegar
¼ cup extra-virgin olive oil
¼ cup chopped chives
Salt and pepper to taste

1. Shave corn kernels from cob, shearing them from the stem end to the tip with a knife. Cook in rapidly boiling salted water for 1 minute.
2. Toss with beans, vinegar, oil, and chives; season to taste.

Ⓥ Italian White Bean and Fresh Herb Salad

Serves 4

COST: $2.59
Per 2 cups
Calories: 279
Fat: 10g
Carbohydrates: 37g
Protein: 12g
Fiber: 13g
Sugar: 7g
Sodium: 279mg

2 14½-ounce cans cannellini beans, drained and rinsed
2 ribs celery, diced
¼ cup chopped fresh parsley
¼ cup chopped fresh basil

2 tablespoons olive oil
3 large tomatoes, chopped
½ cup sliced black olives
2 tablespoons lemon juice
Salt and pepper to taste

1. In a large skillet, combine the beans, celery, parsley, and basil with olive oil. Heat, stirring frequently, over low heat for 3 minutes, until herbs are softened but not cooked.
2. Remove from heat and stir in remaining ingredients, gently tossing to combine. Chill for at least 1 hour before serving.

Color Your Salad

Salads can definitely help you reach the recommended 5 servings of fruits and vegetables per day; however, they can also contain an excess amount of empty calories, with a little of this and a little of that. The best way to create a nutritionally complete salad is to include a protein and at least three different colors of vegetables. Each color provides your body with different phytochemicals, vitamins, and minerals that work in synergy.

Cucumber Cilantro Salad

Serves 3

COST: $2.74

Per 1½ cups
Calories: 110
Fat: 2g
Carbohydrates: 21g
Protein: 12g
Fiber: 4g
Sugar: 10g
Sodium: 23mg

4 cucumbers, diced
2 tomatoes, chopped
½ red onion, diced small
1 cup soy yogurt, plain

1 tablespoon lemon juice
2 tablespoons chopped fresh
  cilantro
Salt and pepper to taste

Toss together all ingredients, stirring well to combine. Chill for at least 2 hours before serving, to allow flavors to marinate. Toss again just before serving.

Ⓥ Dairy-Free Ranch Dressing

Yields 1 cup

COST: $0.34

Per tablespoon
Calories: 57
Fat: 5g
Carbohydrates: 3g
Protein: 1g
Fiber: 0g
Sugar: 1g
Sodium: 83mg

1 cup vegan mayonnaise
¼ cup soy milk
1 teaspoon Dijon mustard
1 tablespoon lemon juice

1 teaspoon onion powder
¾ teaspoon garlic powder
1 tablespoon minced fresh
  chives

Whisk or blend together all ingredients, except chives, until smooth. Stir in chives until well combined.

V Creamy Miso Sesame Dressing

Yields 1 cup

COST: $0.24

Per tablespoon
Calories: 30
Fat: 2g
Carbohydrates: 2g
Protein: 1g
Fiber: 0.5g
Sugar: 0.5g
Sodium: 383mg

¼ cup miso
2 tablespoons rice wine vinegar
¼ cup soy sauce

2 tablespoons sesame oil
½ cup soy milk
2 tablespoons lime juice

Process all ingredients together in a blender or food processor until smooth.

Miso Trivia

Miso is available in a variety of interchangeable flavors and colors with red, white, and barley miso being the most common. It's really a personal preference which type you use.

V Asian Ranch Dressing

Yields ⅔ cup

COST: $0.51

Per tablespoon
Calories: 69
Fat: 6g
Carbohydrates: 4g
Protein: 1.5g
Fiber: 0g
Sugar: 2.5g
Sodium: 383mg

½ cup vegan mayonnaise
⅓ cup rice vinegar
¼ cup soy sauce
2 tablespoons sesame oil
2 teaspoons sugar

½ teaspoon powdered ginger
¾ teaspoon garlic powder
1 tablespoon chopped fresh chives

Combine all ingredients except chives in a blender or food processor until smooth and creamy. Stir in chives by hand.

Ⓥ Thai Orange Peanut Dressing

Yields ¾ cup

COST: $0.12

Per tablespoon
Calories: 37
Fat: 3g
Carbohydrates: 2g
Protein: 1.5g
Fiber: 0.5g
Sugar: 1g
Sodium: 176mg

¼ cup natural peanut butter at room temperature
¼ cup orange juice
2 tablespoons soy sauce
2 tablespoons rice vinegar

2 tablespoons water
½ teaspoon garlic powder
½ teaspoon honey
¼ teaspoon crushed red chili flakes

Whisk together all ingredients until smooth and creamy, adding more or less liquid to achieve desired consistency.

Ⓥ Salad of Celery Root and Pears

Serves 6

COST: $0.79

Per ½ cup salad and pear
Calories: 164
Fat: 12g
Carbohydrates: 13g
Protein: 2g
Fiber: 3g
Sugar: 7g
Sodium: 124mg

1 medium celery root (about the size of a baseball), peeled
¼ cup vegan mayonnaise
½ hard-boiled egg, chopped
1 tablespoon finely chopped Italian (flat-leaf) parsley
2 cornichons (little sour gherkins), finely chopped

2 tablespoons Dijon mustard
Juice of 1 lemon
2 ripe pears (Bartlett and Bosc are great, but choose your own variety)
2 tablespoons extra-virgin olive oil
Salt and freshly ground black pepper

1. Julienne (cut into very thin strips) the celery root. Combine mayonnaise, chopped egg, parsley, cornichons, mustard, lemon juice, and olive oil, and toss with celery root. Season with salt and pepper.
2. Peel pears and slice into 6–8 wedges each. Divide dressed celery root into 6 portions, and garnish with pear slices.

ⓥ Spicy Southwestern Two-Bean Salad

Serves 6

COST: $2.17

Per ¾ cup
Calories: 316
Fat: 17g
Carbohydrates: 33g
Protein: 11g
Fiber: 13g
Sugar: 5g
Sodium: 573mg

1 15-ounce can black beans, drained and rinsed
1 15-ounce can kidney beans, drained and rinsed
1 red bell pepper, chopped
1 large tomato, diced
⅔ cup corn (frozen)
1 red onion, diced

⅓ cup olive oil
¼ cup lime juice
½ teaspoon chili powder
½ teaspoon garlic powder
¼ teaspoon cayenne pepper
½ teaspoon salt
¼ cup chopped fresh cilantro
1 avocado, diced

1. In a large bowl, combine the black beans, kidney beans, bell pepper, tomato, corn, and onion.
2. In a separate small bowl, whisk together the olive oil, lime juice, chili powder, garlic powder, cayenne, and salt.
3. Pour over bean mixture, tossing to coat. Stir in fresh cilantro. Chill for at least 1 hour before serving to allow flavors to mingle. Add avocado and gently toss again just before serving.

Apple and Walnut Salad

Serves 2

COST: $1.44

Per ¾ cup
Calories: 170
Fat: 13g
Carbohydrates: 12g
Protein: 6g
Fiber: 3g
Sugar: 8g
Sodium: 26mg

1 celery stalk
1 cup chopped apple (about 1 small apple)

⅓ cup walnut pieces
2 tablespoons vanilla Greek yogurt

Wash the celery and cut on the diagonal into 1-inch pieces. In a small bowl, combine the celery with the chopped apple and walnut pieces. Toss with the yogurt. Serve immediately, or cover and chill.

Ⓥ Spring Roll Salad

Serves 2

COST: $1.87
Per 1½ cups
Calories: 160
Fat: 3.5g
Carbohydrates: 32g
Protein: 5g
Fiber: 5g
Sugar: 8g
Sodium: 280mg

1 cup mung bean sprouts
1 carrot
1 red bell pepper
1 14-ounce can baby corn

2 teaspoons olive oil
3 teaspoons soy sauce
1 tablespoon red wine vinegar
1 teaspoon granulated sugar

1. Wash the vegetables. Drain the mung bean sprouts thoroughly. Peel the carrot and cut into thin strips about 2 inches long. Cut the red pepper in half, remove the seeds, and cut into thin strips about 2 inches long. Rinse the baby corn in warm water and drain thoroughly.
2. Combine the olive oil, soy sauce, red wine vinegar, and sugar in a jar and shake well. Toss the salad with the dressing. Wait about 30 minutes to serve to allow the flavors to blend.

The Dirty Dozen

A common question is, "Should I buy organic?" Today, people are becoming more aware of the dangers of pesticides and herbicides on and in our foods, but buying organic can be expensive. What's a broke college student to do? The Dirty Dozen list from the Environmental Working Group lists the foods ranked highest in pesticides and herbicides each year. Utilize this list to set your grocery store budget and only buy organic produce for foods on the Dirty Dozen list.

Ⓥ Messy Taco Salad

Serves 4

COST: $2.05
Per 1½ cups
Calories: 207
Fat: 4g
Carbohydrates: 32g
Protein: 10g
Fiber: 10g
Sugar: 8g
Sodium: 862mg

2 heads iceberg lettuce, chopped
½ cup sliced black olives
½ cup corn
1 jalapeño pepper, seeded and sliced

1 can refried black beans
2 tablespoons taco sauce
¼ cup salsa
¼ cup vegan mayonnaise
12 tortilla chips, crumbled
1 avocado, diced

1. Combine the lettuce, olives, corn, and jalapeño pepper in a large bowl.
2. Warm the beans slightly over the stove or in the microwave, just until softened. Combine beans with taco sauce, salsa, and mayonnaise, breaking up the beans and mixing to form a thick sauce.
3. Combine bean mixture with lettuce, stirring to combine as much as possible. Add tortilla chips and avocado, and stir gently to combine. Add a dash or two of extra hot sauce, to taste.

Baked Tortilla Chips

Why not make your own tortilla chips? Slice whole-wheat tortillas into strips or triangles, and arrange in a single layer on a baking sheet. Drizzle with olive oil for a crispier chip, and season with a bit of salt and garlic powder if you want, or just bake them plain. It'll take about 5–6 minutes on each side in a 300°F oven.

V Mixed Baby Greens with Balsamic Vinaigrette

Serves 6

COST: $0.67
Per 1 cup
Calories: 61
Fat: 4g
Carbohydrates: 4g
Protein: 1g
Fiber: 1g
Sugar: 1g
Sodium: 29mg

8 ounces baby mixed greens (mesclun)
1 bunch chives, cut into 2-inch pieces
1 tablespoon balsamic vinegar

2 tablespoons extra-virgin olive oil
1 tablespoon finely chopped shallots
Salt and freshly ground pepper to taste

Wash greens and spin dry; combine with chives. Whisk together the vinegar, oil, and shallots. Toss greens with vinaigrette and season to taste.

V Three-Bean Salad

Serves 6

COST: $1.13
Per 1 cup
Calories: 276
Fat: 12g
Carbohydrates: 31g
Protein: 10g
Fiber: 10g
Sugar: 4g
Sodium: 606mg

1 16-ounce can green beans
1 16-ounce can yellow wax beans
1 16-ounce can red kidney beans
1 onion

2 stevia packets
⅔ cup vinegar
⅓ cup extra-virgin olive oil
½ teaspoon salt
⅛ teaspoon pepper

1. Drain the beans. Slice the onion thinly, then cut the slices into quarters. Whisk together the stevia, vinegar, oil, salt, and pepper. Combine the beans, onions, and dressing, mixing well.
2. Chill at least 4 hours, or overnight, stirring occasionally. If desired, salad can be drained before serving.

Serves 4

COST: $1.06
Per 1 cup
Calories: 238
Fat: 14g
Carbohydrates: 25g
Protein: 6g
Fiber: 5g
Sugar: 3g
Sodium: 97mg

1 pound fresh baby spinach
¼ cup extra-virgin olive oil
1 pound small red potatoes, cut into ½-inch slices, boiled 10 minutes, and drained

1 medium red onion, halved, thinly sliced
20 black olives, pitted
1 tablespoon balsamic vinegar
Salt and pepper to taste

1. Place spinach in a large mixing bowl. Heat olive oil in a large skillet over high heat for 1 minute; add potatoes and onions. Cook over high heat until lightly browned, about 5 minutes. Remove from heat; add olives, vinegar, salt, and pepper.
2. Pour potato mixture over spinach, and invert skillet over bowl to hold in heat. Allow to steam 1 minute, then divide onto 4 plates, arranging potatoes, onions, and olives on top. Serve warm.

Ⓥ Lentil Salad

Serves 8

COST: $0.71
Per ¾ cup
Calories: 241
Fat: 5g
Carbohydrates: 36g
Protein: 14g
Fiber: 7g
Sugar: 2g
Sodium: 8mg

1 pound dried lentils
2 medium onions, finely chopped
3 scallions, chopped
1 green pepper, finely chopped
1 tablespoon toasted cumin powder

Pinch of cayenne pepper
Juice of 1 lemon (about ¼ cup)
2 tablespoons extra-virgin olive oil
Salt and freshly ground black pepper

1. Wash lentils and pick through to take out any stones. Boil in 2 quarts water until tender but not broken up, about 35 minutes
2. Spread on a pan to cool.
3. Combine with onions, scallions, and green pepper. Dress with remaining ingredients, and serve on a bed of dressed baby greens.

Ⓥ Barley and Corn Salad

Serves 8

COST: $0.67	
Per ½ cup	
Calories: 178	
Fat: 4g	
Carbohydrates: 33g	
Protein: 5g	
Fiber: 6g	
Sugar: 1g	
Sodium: 17mg	

1 cup barley
1 pound frozen sweet corn kernels
1 carrot, chopped finely
2 ribs celery, chopped finely
1 medium red onion, chopped finely
1 tablespoon red wine vinegar
2 tablespoons extra-virgin olive oil
½ cup chopped fresh herbs, such as parsley, chives, basil, oregano, mint, and/or cilantro
Salt and freshly ground black pepper to taste

1. Boil the barley in 2 quarts lightly salted water until it is very tender, about 30 minutes. Drain and spread on a platter to cool.
2. Heat a dry cast-iron pan or skillet over a high flame for 1 minute. Add the corn and cook without stirring until some kernels attain a slight char and the corn has a smoky aroma, about 5 minutes.
3. Combine the barley, corn, carrot, celery, and onion in a mixing bowl. Add all remaining ingredients and toss well to coat.

Ⓥ Edamame Salad

Serves 4

COST: $1.09	
Per ¾ cup	
Calories: 313	
Fat: 19g	
Carbohydrates: 21g	
Protein: 17g	
Fiber: 7g	
Sugar: 2g	
Sodium: 201mg	

2 cups frozen shelled edamame, thawed and drained
1 red bell pepper, diced
¾ cup corn kernels
3 tablespoons chopped fresh cilantro
3 tablespoons olive oil
2 tablespoons red wine vinegar
1 teaspoon soy sauce
1 teaspoon chili powder
2 teaspoons lemon juice
Salt and pepper to taste

1. Combine edamame, bell pepper, corn, and cilantro in a large bowl.
2. Whisk together the olive oil, vinegar, soy sauce, chili powder, and lemon or lime juice, and combine with the edamame. Add salt and pepper to taste.
3. Chill for at least 1 hour before serving.

Sweet Red Salad with Strawberries and Beets

Serves 4

COST: $1.89

Per 1½ cups
Calories: 295
Fat: 24g
Carbohydrates: 25g
Protein: 4g
Fiber: 5g
Sugar: 18g
Sodium: 73mg

4 small beets, peeled and
  chopped
4 cups water for boiling
4 cups spinach
1 cup sliced strawberries
½ cup chopped pecans

¼ cup olive oil
2 tablespoons red wine vinegar
2 tablespoons agave nectar
2 tablespoons orange juice
Salt and pepper to taste

1. Boil beets in water until soft, about 20 minutes. Allow to cool completely.
2. In a large bowl, combine spinach, strawberries, pecans, and cooled beets.
3. In a separate small bowl, whisk together the olive oil, vinegar, agave nectar, and orange juice, and pour over salad, tossing well to coat.
4. Season with salt and pepper to taste.

Ⓥ Kidney Bean and Chickpea Salad

Serves 6

COST: $0.41

Per ¾ cup
Calories: 252
Fat: 12g
Carbohydrates: 8g
Protein: 7g
Fiber: 8g
Sugar: 5g
Sodium: 569mg

¼ cup olive oil
¼ cup red wine vinegar
½ teaspoon paprika
2 tablespoons lemon juice
1 14-ounce can chickpeas,
  drained
1 14-ounce can kidney beans,
  drained

½ cup sliced black olives
1 8-ounce can corn, drained
½ red onion, chopped
1 tablespoon chopped fresh
  parsley
Salt and pepper to taste

1. Whisk together olive oil, vinegar, paprika, and lemon juice.
2. In a large bowl, combine the chickpeas, beans, olives, corn, red onion, and parsley. Pour the olive oil dressing over the bean mixture and toss well to combine.
3. Season with salt and pepper to taste.
4. Chill for at least 1 hour before serving to allow flavors to mingle.

Ⓥ Marinated Beet Salad

Serves 6

COST: $0.41

Per ⅓ cup
Calories: 78
Fat: 4g
Carbohydrates: 8g
Protein: 1.5g
Fiber: 3g
Sugar: 5g
Sodium: 61mg

Dressing

1 tablespoon rice wine vinegar
2 tablespoons extra-virgin olive oil
¼ teaspoon dried oregano leaves
¼ teaspoon dried basil leaves
½ teaspoon freshly chopped parsley
1 teaspoon finely chopped shallots
Salt and pepper to taste

Salad

1 pound fresh beets, stem end trimmed
1 tablespoon red wine vinegar
6 large romaine lettuce leaves, washed

1. Boil beets in a small saucepan with red wine vinegar and enough water to cover. Cook until tender, about 30 minutes. Chill, then peel and cut into ¼-inch slices.
2. In a bowl, combine rice wine vinegar, olive oil, oregano, basil, parsley, and shallots. Season with salt and pepper.
3. Add beets, and marinate 10–15 minutes. Place lettuce leaves on 6 plates, trimming stem end to fit inside rim. Arrange beets in an overlapping pattern atop lettuce leaves, and drizzle with remaining marinade.

Classic Waldorf Salad

Serves 2

COST: $1.10

Per 1¼ cup
Calories: 330
Fat: 24g
Carbohydrates: 27g
Protein: 5g
Fiber: 4g
Sugar: 8g
Sodium: 140mg

1 celery stalk
1½ cups chopped red apple
½ cup walnut pieces
1 tablespoon honey

2 tablespoons vegan
  mayonnaise
1½ teaspoons lemon juice

1. Wash the celery and cut diagonally into 1-inch slices. In a serving dish, mix the celery with the apple and the walnuts.
2. Mix the honey into the mayonnaise to form a creamy dressing. Stir in the lemon juice.
3. Toss the celery mixture with the dressing. Chill until ready to serve.

Ⓥ Sesame and Soy Coleslaw Salad

Serves 4

COST: $0.65

Per 1 cup
Calories: 121
Fat: 7g
Carbohydrates: 12g
Protein: 1g
Fiber: 4g
Sugar: 9g
Sodium: 169mg

1 head Napa cabbage,
  shredded
1 carrot, grated
2 green onions, chopped
1 red bell pepper, sliced thin
2 tablespoons olive oil

2 tablespoons apple cider
  vinegar
2 teaspoons soy sauce
½ teaspoon sesame oil
2 tablespoons maple syrup
2 tablespoons sesame seeds

1. Toss together the cabbage, carrot, green onions, and bell pepper in a large bowl.
2. In a separate small bowl, whisk together the olive oil, vinegar, soy sauce, sesame oil, and maple syrup until well combined.
3. Drizzle dressing over cabbage and veggies, add sesame seeds, and toss well to combine.

Raspberry Vinaigrette

Yields 1¼ cups

COST: $0.18

Per tablespoon
Calories: 87
Fat: 8g
Carbohydrates: 10g
Protein: 0g
Fiber: 0g
Sugar: 9g
Sodium: 19mg

¼ cup balsamic vinegar
2 tablespoons lime juice
¼ cup raspberry preserves
2 tablespoons Dijon mustard

½ teaspoon sugar
¾ cup olive oil
Salt and pepper to taste

1. Process together vinegar, lime juice, raspberry preserves, mustard, and sugar in a food processor or blender until smooth.
2. Slowly add olive oil, just a few drops at a time, on high speed to allow oil to emulsify.
3. Season with salt and pepper.

Ⓥ Asian Cucumber Salad

Serves 4

COST: $0.45

Per tablespoon
Calories: 21
Fat: 1g
Carbohydrates: 4g
Protein: 0g
Fiber: 0.5g
Sugar: 2g
Sodium: 2mg

¼ cup rice wine vinegar
1 teaspoon sugar
1 teaspoon chopped jalapeño
  pepper

1 large cucumber
Sesame oil

1. Whisk together rice vinegar, sugar, and chopped jalapeño. Peel cucumber and halve lengthwise; remove seeds. Slice seeded cucumber very thinly into half-moons. Combine with dressing, drizzle in a few drops of sesame oil, and toss to coat.
2. Marinate for at least 10 minutes before serving.

Southeast Asian Slaw

Serves 4

COST: $0.43

Per 1 cup
Calories: 37
Fat: 1.5g
Carbohydrates: 6g
Protein: 1g
Fiber: 2g
Sugar: 3g
Sodium: 307mg

¼ head (about ½ pound) Napa cabbage
½ carrot, grated
1 small red onion, julienned
1 small Thai chili, finely chopped
¼ cup chopped cilantro

Juice of 1 lime
1 tablespoon rice wine vinegar
1 teaspoon sugar
1 teaspoon coconut oil
A few drops sesame oil
½ teaspoon salt

1. Shred the cabbage as fine as you possibly can, using a knife, mandoline, or slicing machine. Combine with carrot, onion, chili pepper, and cilantro.
2. Dress with lime, rice vinegar, sugar, coconut oil, sesame oil, and salt; toss thoroughly.
3. Refrigerate for at least 30 minutes before serving.

Ⓥ Summer Vegetable Slaw

Serves 8

COST: $0.82

Per 1 cup
Calories: 85
Fat: 2g
Carbohydrates: 15g
Protein: 3g
Fiber: 3.5g
Sugar: 5g
Sodium: 22mg

1 small head Napa cabbage (about 1 pound)
2 carrots, peeled
¼ pound snow peas
1 each red, yellow, and green bell peppers, seeded
12 green beans
1 small red onion

2 ears fresh sweet corn, shucked
½ teaspoon sugar
¼ cup cider vinegar
1 tablespoon vegetable oil (preferably peanut oil)
Pinch of celery seeds
Salt and black pepper to taste

1. Quarter and core the cabbage; slice as thinly as possible. Using a swivel peeler, shave carrot into as many paper-thin curls as you can. Discard or save remaining carrot for another use. Cut carrot curls, snow peas, bell peppers, green beans, and onion into fine julienne. Cut corn kernels from the cob.
2. Combine all vegetables in a large mixing bowl; dress with sugar, vinegar, oil, celery seeds, salt, and pepper. Allow to sit at least 10 minutes before serving. This is an excellent accompaniment to crispy fried foods like beer-battered onion rings.

ⓥ Tangerine and Mint Salad

Serves 2

COST: $2.47

Per 2 cups
Calories: 322
Fat: 26g
Carbohydrates: 22g
Protein: 3g
Fiber: 6g
Sugar: 13g
Sodium: 55mg

1 head green lettuce, chopped
2 tablespoons chopped fresh
   mint
2 tangerines, sectioned
⅓ cup chopped walnuts

1 bulb fennel, sliced thin
2 tablespoons olive oil
Salt and pepper to taste

Gently toss together the lettuce, mint, tangerines, walnuts, and sliced fennel. Drizzle with olive oil, salt, and pepper.

Tomato and Bread Salad (Panzanella)

Serves 4

COST: $2.92

Per 1 cup
Calories: 107
Fat: 5.5g
Carbohydrates: 12g
Protein: 3g
Fiber: 2g
Sugar: 3g
Sodium: 393mg

2 cups diced (½-inch) ripe red
   tomatoes, any variety
¼ cup finely chopped red onion
½ teaspoon salt
1½ tablespoons extra-virgin
   olive oil
2 teaspoons fresh lemon juice

2 cups day-old bakery bread,
   cut into ½-inch cubes, air-
   dried overnight or baked 20
   minutes at 325°F
¼ cup roughly chopped Italian
   parsley
Black pepper to taste

1. Dress tomatoes and chopped onion with salt, olive oil, and lemon juice.
2. Toss gently with dried bread cubes and parsley.
3. Season with freshly ground black pepper.

Tatsoi Salad with Orange-Sesame Vinaigrette

Serves 4

6 cups tatsoi (Japanese baby spinach leaves)
¼ cup Orange-Sesame Vinaigrette (see recipe in this chapter)

½ cup red Bermuda onion, sliced paper-thin

1. Wash and spin the tatsoi leaves, then toss gently with half of the dressing. Distribute onto 4 salad plates.
2. Arrange sliced onions atop each salad, and finish with a final spoonful of dressing.

Orange-Sesame Vinaigrette

Yields about 1¼ cups

Zest of ½ orange
Zest of ½ lime
1 pickled jalapeño pepper, chopped, plus 1 tablespoon of the brine it came in (usually found near the olives in supermarkets)
¼ cup Japanese rice wine vinegar

¼ cup orange juice concentrate
1½ teaspoons Dijon mustard
A few drops sesame oil (about ⅛ teaspoon)
¼ cup peanut oil
¼ cup olive oil
Salt and freshly ground black pepper

1. Combine zests, pickled jalapeño and brine, rice wine vinegar, orange juice concentrate, Dijon, and sesame oil in a blender.
2. Blend on medium speed, slowly drizzling in the peanut and olive oils. Season to taste with salt and pepper.

ⓥ California Garden Salad with Avocado and Sprouts

Serves 4

COST: $4.99
Per 2 cups
Calories: 194
Fat: 17g
Carbohydrates: 9g
Protein: 3g
Fiber: 5g
Sugar: 3g
Sodium: 306mg

Dressing

1 tablespoon fresh-squeezed
lemon juice
3 tablespoons extra-virgin
olive oil
1 tablespoon finely chopped
shallots
½ teaspoon salt
¼ teaspoon freshly ground
black pepper

Salad

2 heads Bibb lettuce
2 ripe tomatoes, cored, cut into
8 wedges each
1 ripe avocado
1 cup alfalfa sprouts

1. Make the dressing: Combine the lemon juice, olive oil, shallots, salt, and pepper in a small bowl, mixing well.
2. Arrange lettuce leaves, stem-end in, onto 4 plates, making flower-petal pattern. Inner leaves will be too small, so reserve them for another use.
3. Toss tomatoes in 1 tablespoon dressing; place 4 onto each salad. Peel avocado, cut into 8 wedges, and toss with 1 tablespoon dressing. Place 2 wedges on each salad. Divide sprouts into 4 bunches, and place a bunch in the center of each salad. Drizzle salads with remaining dressing, or serve on the side.

Ⓥ Madras Curry Dressing

Yields about 1¼ cups

COST: $0.19

Per tablespoon
Calories: 90
Fat: 9g
Carbohydrates: 1.5g
Protein: 0g
Fiber: 0.5g
Sugar: 0.5g
Sodium: 63mg

1 tablespoon oil
1 small red onion, finely chopped
2 tablespoons chopped red bell pepper
1 teaspoon finely chopped and seeded jalapeño pepper
2 tablespoons Madras curry powder
1 teaspoon ground coriander

1 teaspoon ground turmeric
1 tablespoon raisins, soaked in ½ cup warm water
¼ teaspoon cayenne pepper
Juice of 1 lime (about 2 tablespoons)
1 cup vegan mayonnaise
2 tablespoons chopped cilantro
Salt and pepper to taste

1. In a small skillet, heat oil over medium heat for 1 minute. Add onions, bell pepper, and jalapeño. Cook until onions are translucent, about 2 minutes; add curry powder, coriander, and turmeric. Cook 4 minutes more, stirring with a wooden spoon. Some of the spices may stick—this is not a problem. Remove from heat; allow to cool a few minutes. Drain the raisins.
2. In the bowl of a food processor, combine onion mixture and raisins. Pulse until smooth, scraping sides of bowl frequently. Add half of lime juice and the mayonnaise. Pulse to combine, then stir in cilantro. Adjust seasoning with salt, pepper, and remaining lime juice. Can be made up to 1 week in advance.

Insalata Caprese (Tomato-Mozzarella Salad)

Serves 4

COST: $2.89

Per 1 tomato
Calories: 196
Fat: 13g
Carbohydrates: 10g
Protein: 11g
Fiber: 3.5g
Sugar: 5g
Sodium: 160mg

4 large, ripe red tomatoes
16 oz. fresh mozzarella ball
8 top sprigs of fresh basil
2 tablespoons extra-virgin olive oil

Coarse (kosher) salt and freshly ground black pepper

1. Slice each tomato into 4 thick slices, discarding the polar ends. Cut mozzarella ball into 6 even slices. Shingle alternating tomato and mozzarella slices onto 4 plates, starting and ending with tomato slices.
2. Garnish with 2 sprigs basil each, and drizzle olive oil over all. Sprinkle with salt and a few grinds of black pepper. Serve immediately.

Serves 8

COST: $0.89

Per 1 cup
Calories: 198
Fat: 17g
Carbohydrates: 6g
Protein: 5g
Fiber: 2g
Sugar: 1g
Sodium: 294mg

Dressing

1 egg yolk
1 tablespoon Dijon mustard
Juice of ½ lemon (about 2
  tablespoons)
2 cloves garlic, finely chopped
½ cup vegetable oil (preferably
  peanut oil)
¼ cup grated Parmigiano-
  Reggiano cheese
Pinch of cayenne pepper
Salt and pepper

Salad

1 head romaine lettuce,
  washed, torn into bite-sized
  pieces
1 cup croutons
1 small wedge Parmigiano-
  Reggiano cheese

1. Make the dressing: In a mixing bowl or food processor, combine the egg yolk, mustard, lemon juice, and garlic. Vigorously whisk or process in the oil, starting just a drop at a time and gradually drizzling it in a small stream, until all is emulsified into a smooth mayonnaise. Stir in the cheese, cayenne, salt, pepper, and a little extra lemon if desired.
2. Toss the lettuce and croutons with the dressing, and divide onto 8 plates, arranging croutons on top. If desired, shave curls of Parmigiano-Reggiano over each salad, using a vegetable peeler. Dressing may be made up to 1 week in advance.

CHAPTER 5

Side Dishes

You may think that side dishes are not that important, but what's a meal without sides like Garlic Bread, Roasted-Garlic Mashed Potatoes, or Caramelized Baby Carrots? Boring! That's what! Sides really can make the meal—and the sides found in this chapter put the limp carrots and blanched broccoli served at your school's dining hall to shame! As a vegetarian, vegetables should fill at least half your plate in order for your body to receive an adequate amount of vitamin and minerals like vitamins B_{12}, A, C, and K and iron, calcium, and zinc. These side dishes are guaranteed to turn these dull veggies into something you can't live without!

Maple Baked Beans

Serves 6

COST: $0.57
Per ½ cup
Calories: 228
Fat: 1g
Carbohydrates: 49g
Protein: 8g
Fiber: 8g
Sugar: 26g
Sodium: 436mg

3 cups navy beans
9 cups water
1 onion, chopped
½ cup maple syrup
¼ cup barbecue sauce
2 tablespoons molasses

1 tablespoon Dijon mustard
1 tablespoon chili powder
1 teaspoon paprika
½ teaspoon salt
¾ teaspoon pepper

1. Cover beans in water and allow to soak at least 8 hours or overnight. Drain.
2. Preheat oven to 350°F.
3. In a large Dutch oven or sturdy pot, combine beans and remaining ingredients. Bring to a rolling boil on the stove. Cover and bake beans for 1½ hours, stirring once or twice. Uncover and cook 1 more hour. Alternatively, beans can be simmered over low heat for 1½–2 hours on the stovetop.

Ⓥ Smoky Spiced Collard Greens with Turnip

Serves 4

COST: $0.74
Per serving
Calories: 65
Fat: 4g
Carbohydrates: 7.5g
Protein: 3g
Fiber: 3g
Sugar: 3g
Sodium: 326mg

1 bunch collard greens
1 medium white turnip, peeled
   and diced into ¼-inch pieces
1 medium onion, chopped
1 chipotle chili, dried, cut in
   half

1 tablespoon olive oil
½ teaspoon salt
1 cup vegetable stock

1. Wash greens and remove the stems. Cut leaves into long thin strips (julienne).
2. In a heavy-bottomed pot, sauté the turnip, onion, and chili in olive oil until the onion is translucent. Add the greens and salt, and sauté a few minutes more, until greens are wilted.
3. Add stock or water, bring to a boil, and reduce heat to simmer for 20 minutes, or until greens are very tender and turnips are soft.

Ⓥ Mexican Frijoles Refritos (Refried Beans)

Serves 6

COST: $0.79

Per serving
Calories: 158
Fat: 14g
Carbohydrates: 23g
Protein: 2g
Fiber: 2g
Sugar: 1g
Sodium: 203mg

½ pound pinto beans, washed
¼ white onion, roughly
   chopped

6 tablespoons olive oil
½ teaspoon salt
½ cup chopped white onion

1. Prepare the beans: Bring beans to a boil with onions, oil, salt, and 5 cups water in a 2½-quart pot. Lower flame and simmer 2½–3 hours, until very tender, skimming occasionally and adding water if necessary to keep it brothy.

2. Fry the beans (about 4 cups cooked beans with broth): Cook the onions in the oil until translucent in a 10-inch skillet (iron is best), then add the beans (broth included) 1 cup at a time, mashing with a wooden spoon over high heat. Constantly mash and stir until beans dry out and sizzle around the edges. They should start coming away from the surface of the pan. Rock the pan back and forth to make sure they loosen, and turn them out, omelet style, onto a warm serving platter.

3. Garnish with radishes, lettuce, shredded queso blanco (a fresh Mexican cheese sold in most Hispanic food sections), or feta cheese. Accompany with Mexican Rice (see Chapter 6).

Serves 2

COST: $2.64

Per 2 cups
Calories: 190
Fat: 4.5g
Carbohydrates: 31g
Protein: 10g
Fiber: 10
Sugar: 11g
Sodium: 390mg

1 red bell pepper
1 orange bell pepper
3 packed cups fresh spinach
  leaves
2 tomatoes
1 cup canned chickpeas,
  drained

4 tablespoons red wine vinegar
2 teaspoons lemon juice
1 teaspoon extra-virgin olive oil
⅛ teaspoon (or to taste) garlic
  powder

1. Wash the bell peppers and pat dry. Wash the spinach leaves and drain thoroughly. Wash the tomatoes and slice.
2. Place a sheet of aluminum foil on a roasting pan. Broil the peppers for 10 minutes or until the skins are blackened. Turn the peppers over after 5 minutes so that both sides blacken.
3. Remove from oven, place in a plastic bag, and seal. Leave the peppers in the bag for at least 10 minutes. Remove the skin from the blackened peppers, cut them in half, and remove the seeds.
4. Cut the peppers into long strips and let sit for 2–3 hours. Wipe the strips dry and cut into cubes.
5. Toss the chickpeas with the red wine vinegar, lemon juice, olive oil, and garlic powder. Add the roasted pepper cubes, spinach, and sliced tomatoes. Serve immediately.

Ⓥ Roasted Brussels Sprouts with Apples

Serves 4

COST: $0.76

Per ¼ recipe
Calories: 133
Fat: 7g
Carbohydrates: 17g
Protein: 2g
Fiber: 4g
Sugar: 10g
Sodium: 451mg

2 cups Brussels sprouts,
   chopped into quarters
8 whole cloves garlic, peeled
2 tablespoons olive oil

2 tablespoons balsamic
   vinegar
¾ teaspoon salt
½ teaspoon black pepper
2 apples, cored and chopped

1. Preheat oven to 425°F.
2. Arrange Brussels sprouts and garlic in a single layer on a baking sheet. Drizzle with olive oil and balsamic vinegar and season with salt and pepper. Roast for 10–12 minutes, tossing once.
3. Remove tray from oven and add apples, tossing gently to combine, then roast for 10 more minutes or until apples are soft, tossing once again.

Reuse and Recycle!

Recycle this basic recipe by adding an extra garnish or two each time you make it. Try it with a touch of fresh rosemary, a couple of shakes of a vegan Parmesan cheese, some chopped toasted nuts, or vegetarian bacon bits for crunch!

ⓥ Spinach with Pine Nuts and Garlic

Serves 4

COST: $2.60

Per ¼ recipe
Calories: 207
Fat: 16g
Carbohydrates: 13g
Protein: 8g
Fiber: 7g
Sugar: 1.5g
Sodium: 335mg

¼ cup pine nuts (pignolia)
2 tablespoons extra-virgin
    olive oil
2 cloves garlic, finely chopped

2 pounds washed spinach
    leaves, stems removed
½ teaspoon salt and freshly
    ground black pepper
Lemon

1. Gently toast the nuts in a dry sauté pan over medium heat until they start to brown. Set aside.
2. In a very large pan, heat the olive oil and garlic over medium heat until it sizzles and starts to brown.
3. Add ⅓ of the spinach and the pine nuts, and sauté until spinach is wilted and lets off some liquid. Add the rest of the spinach in batches, seasoning with salt and pepper as it cooks. Serve with lemon wedges.

The Incredible Shrinking Spinach!

Leafy green vegetables look huge when they're taking up cubic yards of refrigerator space, but seem to shrivel into mouse-sized portions (actually to one-sixth their raw volume) when you cook them. Stem trimmage also means they're less voluminous than you'd think. Figure on a half pound of raw greens per person (slightly less if the stems are eaten, as with Swiss chard).

Ⓥ Sautéed Mushrooms

Serves 2

COST: $0.52

Per ½ recipe
Calories: 69
Fat: 7g
Carbohydrates: 1.5g
Protein: 1.5g
Fiber: 0.5g
Sugar: 1g
Sodium: 4mg

3 ounces fresh button
  mushrooms
1 tablespoon olive oil

⅛ teaspoon (or to taste) chili
  powder

1. Clean the mushrooms with a damp cloth. Slice thinly and cut off the stems if desired.
2. Heat the olive oil in the frying pan. Lay the mushrooms flat in the pan. Cook on medium heat until most of the oil is absorbed, about 3–5 minutes.
3. Stir in the chili powder. Cook the mushrooms on medium-high heat, stirring frequently, for 2–3 minutes or until browned. Serve hot.

Ⓥ Steamed Broccoli

Serves 2

COST: $0.99

Per 2 ounces
Calories: 30
Fat: 0g
Carbohydrates: 6g
Protein: 3g
Fiber: 3g
Sugar: 0g
Sodium: 30mg

4 ounces broccoli
Water, as needed

1. Wash the broccoli and drain. Chop the broccoli into bite-sized pieces.
2. Fill a medium-sized saucepan with 1 inch of water. Place a metal steamer inside the pan. Make sure the water is not touching the bottom of the steamer. Heat the water to boiling.
3. When the water is boiling, add the broccoli pieces to the steamer. Cover and steam until the broccoli is tender, about 10 minutes. Drain and serve.

Broccoli Florets with Lemon Butter Sauce

Serves 4

COST: $1.55

Per 1 cup
Calories: 225
Fat: 17g
Carbohydrates: 13g
Protein: 5g
Fiber: 4g
Sugar: 3g
Sodium: 84mg

2 small shallots, finely chopped
¼ cup white cooking wine
Juice of 1 lemon
3 ounces cold, unsalted butter, cut into small pieces

Salt and white pepper
1 large head broccoli, broken into florets

1. Place the shallots, wine, and half of the lemon juice in a small saucepan over medium heat. Simmer until almost dry. Reduce heat to very low, and stir in a few small pieces of butter, swirling it in with a wire whisk until it is mostly melted.
2. Gradually add the remaining butter, whisking constantly, until all is used and sauce is smooth. Never boil. Season the sauce with salt, white pepper, and remaining lemon juice to taste. Keep in a warm place, but not over a flame.
3. Wash the broccoli and boil in 4 quarts of rapidly boiling, salted water. Drain, and serve with lemon butter sauce.

Ⓥ Microwave Green Beans

Serves 2

COST: $0.86

Per 2 ounces
Calories: 30
Fat: 0g
Carbohydrates: 7g
Protein: 3g
Fiber: 2g
Sugar: 1g
Sodium: 135mg

3½ ounces fresh green beans
⅓ cup vegetable stock

1. Rinse the green beans under cold, running water. Drain and pat dry.
2. Place the green beans in a microwave-safe bowl and cover with the vegetable broth.
3. Cook on high heat for 1½–2 minutes, or until they are crisp and bright green. Serve with butter, margarine, or soy sauce if desired.

Fruity Snow Peas

Serves 3

COST: $1.02

Per ½ cup
Calories: 80
Fat: 0g
Carbohydrates: 13g
Protein: 2g
Fiber: 2g
Sugar: 5g
Sodium: 10mg

6 ounces fresh snow peas
½ cup canned fruit cocktail
  juice

1. Rinse the snow peas under cold, running water. Drain and pat dry. Trim the ends.
2. Place the snow peas in a shallow, microwave-safe bowl and add the fruit cocktail juice.
3. Microwave on high heat for 1½–2 minutes or until the snow peas are crisp and bright green. Serve hot or chilled.

Ⓥ Oven-Roasted Mushrooms

Serves 4

COST: $1.35

Per ½ cup
Calories: 76
Fat: 4g
Carbohydrates: 9g
Protein: 3g
Fiber: 3.5g
Sugar: 0g
Sodium: 313mg

1 pound cremini mushrooms
1 tablespoon extra-virgin olive
  oil
1 teaspoon dried thyme
½ teaspoon salt

Pinch of crushed red pepper
  flakes
1 cup Italian parsley, chopped
1 teaspoon balsamic vinegar

1. Preheat oven to 400°F.
2. In a bowl, combine mushrooms, olive oil, thyme, salt, and red pepper flakes; toss to coat.
3. Spread in a single layer into a roasting pan. Roast in center of oven for 30 minutes, until nicely browned.
4. Toss with parsley and vinegar. Serve hot or at room temperature.

Ⓥ Corn on the Cob

Serves 1

COST: $0.89
Per 1 ear of corn
Calories: 120
Fat: 1g
Carbohydrates: 27g
Protein: 5g
Fiber: 3.5g
Sugar: 4g
Sodium: 6mg

1 ear corn

1. Remove the husk from the corn. Wrap the corn in wax paper and place on a paper towel or microwave-safe dish.
2. Microwave on high heat for 2–3 minutes. Let stand in microwave for a few minutes. Serve with salt and butter if desired.

Ⓥ Basic Peas

Serves 1

COST: $0.41
Per 1 cup
Calories: 110
Fat: 0.5g
Carbohydrates: 20g
Protein: 8g
Fiber: 7g
Sugar: 8g
Sodium: 8mg

½ cup water
1 cup frozen peas

Bring the water to a boil. Add the peas and cook until they turn a bright color and are tender (3–5 minutes). Drain and serve.

Homemade Creamed Corn

Serves 2

COST: $0.62

Per ½ cup
Calories: 148
Fat: 6g
Carbohydrates: 21g
Protein: 7g
Fiber: 2g
Sugar: 3g
Sodium: 82mg

1 tablespoon vegan margarine
1 cup frozen corn niblets
¼ cup skim milk

1 teaspoon granulated sugar
Salt and pepper, to taste
1 teaspoon cornstarch

1. Melt the margarine over low heat in a medium-sized saucepan.
2. Add the corn, milk, sugar, and salt and pepper. Increase heat to medium and bring to a boil, stirring constantly. Reduce heat to low and simmer for 5 more minutes, stirring throughout.
3. Push the corn off to the sides of the pan. Increase heat to medium high and add the cornstarch to the liquid in the middle of the pan, stirring constantly until thickened. Make sure there are no lumps. Stir the corn and milk a few times. Serve hot.

Ⓥ Dairy-Free Creamed Spinach and Mushrooms

Serves 4

COST: $1.26

Per ¾ cup
Calories: 164
Fat: 11g
Carbohydrates: 11g
Protein: 8g
Fiber: 4.5g
Sugar: 2g
Sodium: 191mg

½ onion, diced
2 cloves garlic, minced
1½ cups sliced mushrooms
2 tablespoons olive oil
1 tablespoon flour

2 bunches fresh spinach,
    trimmed
1 cup soy milk
1 tablespoon vegan margarine
¼ teaspoon nutmeg
Salt and pepper, to taste

1. Sauté onion, garlic, and mushrooms in olive oil for 3–4 minutes. Add flour and heat, stirring constantly, for 1 minute.
2. Reduce heat to medium low and add spinach and soy milk. Cook uncovered for 8–10 minutes until spinach is soft and liquid has reduced.
3. Stir in remaining ingredients and season with salt and pepper to taste.

ⓥ Roasted-Garlic Mashed Potatoes

Serves 6

COST: $0.57

Per ¾ cup
Calories: 241
Fat: 8g
Carbohydrates: 36g
Protein: 5g
Fiber: 5g
Sugar: 2g
Sodium: 65mg

1 whole head garlic
2 tablespoons olive oil
6 potatoes, cooked

2 tablespoons vegan margarine
½ cup soy creamer
Sea salt and pepper to taste

1. Preheat oven to 400°F.
2. Remove outer layer of skin from garlic head. Drizzle generously with olive oil, wrap in aluminum foil, and place on a baking sheet. Roast in oven for 30 minutes. Gently press cloves out of the skins, and mash smooth with a fork.
3. Using a mixer or a potato masher, combine roasted garlic with potatoes, margarine, and creamer until smooth or desired consistency. Season generously with salt and pepper.

Vegan Mashed Potato Tricks

There's nothing wrong with just switching the butter and milk for vegan versions in your favorite potato recipe, but half a container of nondairy sour cream or cream cheese, a few teaspoons of fresh crumbled sage, or some chopped artichoke hearts will make your spuds come alive. You can also simply add a shake of nutmeg or rosemary.

Simple Vegetarian Stir-Fry

Serves 1

COST: $1.26

Per 1 recipe
Calories: 80
Fat: 4.5g
Carbohydrates: 8g
Protein: 3g
Fiber: 4g
Sugar: 2g
Sodium: 288mg

2 teaspoons coconut oil
1 cup frozen stir-fry vegetable mix

2 tablespoons prepared stir-fry sauce (low sodium)

Heat the coconut oil in a frying pan. Add the frozen vegetables. Cook, stirring continually, over medium to medium-high heat for at least 5 minutes or until the vegetables are brightly colored and tender. Stir in the stir-fry sauce. Mix through and serve hot.

Orange and Ginger Mixed-Veggie Stir-Fry

Serves 4

COST: $1.25

Per 1½ cups
Calories: 156
Fat: 7g
Carbohydrates: 20g
Protein: 6g
Fiber: 5 g
Sugar: 8g
Sodium: 517mg

3 tablespoons orange juice
1 tablespoon apple cider vinegar
2 tablespoons soy sauce
2 tablespoons water
1 tablespoon maple syrup
1 teaspoon powdered ginger

2 cloves garlic, minced
2 tablespoons oil
1 bunch broccoli, chopped
½ cup sliced mushrooms
½ cup snap peas, chopped
1 carrot, sliced
1 cup chopped cabbage

1. Whisk together the orange juice, vinegar, soy sauce, water, maple syrup, and ginger.
2. Heat garlic in oil and add veggies. Allow to cook, stirring frequently, over high heat for 2–3 minutes until just starting to get tender.
3. Add sauce and reduce heat. Simmer, stirring frequently, for another 3–4 minutes, or until veggies are cooked.

V Baked Peppers and Onions

Serves 4

COST: $0.35

Per 1 cup
Calories: 176
Fat: 7g
Carbohydrates: 26g
Protein: 3.5g
Fiber: 4.5 g
Sugar: 5.5g
Sodium: 12mg

5 medium green bell peppers
   (about 1½ pounds)
1 pound small red potatoes
1 large yellow onion

¼ cup extra-virgin olive oil
Kosher salt and freshly ground
   black pepper

1. Preheat oven to 425°F. Wash the peppers and cut into 2-inch pieces. Scrub the potatoes and cut into 1 inch-slices or chunks. Peel the onion and cut into chunks. Place everything into a shallow ovenproof dish; pour the olive oil over the vegetables; toss to coat.
2. Sprinkle with the salt and lots of pepper. Bake for about 30 minutes, until the potatoes are tender.

Braised Swiss Chard

Serves 4

COST: $0.55

Per ¾ cup
Calories: 64
Fat: 6g
Carbohydrates: 2g
Protein: 1g
Fiber: 1g
Sugar: 0g
Sodium: 22mg

1 large bunch Swiss chard
   (about 1½ pounds)
1 cup strong vegetable stock
Salt and freshly ground black
   pepper to taste

1 tablespoon olive oil
2 medium shallots, finely
   chopped (about ¼ cup)
1 tablespoon unsalted butter
Lemon wedges

1. Wash the chard thoroughly under running water, and shake dry. Using your hands, tear the leafy parts away from the stems; set aside. Cut the stems into bite-sized pieces. In a non-Teflon coated skillet bring the stock to a boil; add the stem pieces. Season with salt and pepper; cook until tender. Transfer them to a bowl or plate, reserving their cooking liquid. Wipe out the skillet.
2. Return the skillet to the heat and add the olive oil and shallots. Cook 1 minute until they sizzle and soften slightly. Add the chard leaves, and cook only until they wilt. Add back the stems, plus 2 tablespoons of their cooking liquid. Bring to a simmer, and swirl in the butter.
3. Taste for seasoning. Serve with lemon wedges.

Ⓥ Sweetened Roast Squash

Serves 4

COST: $0.44

Per 1 piece of squash
Calories: 123
Fat: 0g
Carbohydrates: 31g
Protein: 1.5g
Fiber: 3g
Sugar: 16g
Sodium: 302mg

1 butternut squash
½ teaspoon sea salt
4 tablespoons orange juice

4 tablespoons maple syrup
Nutmeg or ginger to taste

1. Preheat oven to 400°F.
2. Chop squash in fourths, and scrape out seeds. Place in a large casserole dish. Sprinkle each chunk of squash with a bit of sea salt, 1 teaspoon orange juice, and 1 tablespoon maple syrup, then a shake of nutmeg or ginger.
3. Cover with foil and bake for 40–45 minutes until squash is soft, basting with any extra sauce once or twice. Serve with grains and protein for a balanced meal.

Easy Roasted Squash Sides

Tossing squash in the oven couldn't be easier. A drizzle of olive oil and a dash of garlic powder, salt, nutritional yeast, and perhaps a touch of cayenne will produce a satisfying roasted squash for a side dish you don't need to sweat over.

Ⓥ Roasted Yukon Gold Potatoes

Serves 4

COST: $0.48

Per ¾ cup
Calories: 192
Fat: 7g
Carbohydrates: 30g
Protein: 3g
Fiber: 5g
Sugar: 3g
Sodium: 308mg

1 medium onion, roughly
  chopped
2 tablespoons olive oil
¼ cup chopped parsley
4 cloves garlic, minced

1½ pounds Yukon Gold potatoes, washed, sliced ½-inch
  thick
½ teaspoon salt
¼ teaspoon pepper

1. Preheat oven to 425°F. Put onion, olive oil, parsley, and garlic in blender or food processor, and purée until smooth. Toss with potatoes and salt, then wrap in a ready-made foil oven bag or a sheet of foil crimped to seal. Potatoes should be no more than 2 layers deep.
2. Bake on a sheet pan in center rack for 45 minutes, until potatoes are tender when poked with a fork. Season with pepper.

Ⓥ Caramelized Baby Carrots

Serves 4

COST: $0.53

Per 1 cup
Calories: 103
Fat: 5g
Carbohydrates: 12g
Protein: 1g
Fiber: 3g
Sugar: 8g
Sodium: 302mg

4 cups baby carrots
1 teaspoon lemon juice
2 tablespoons vegan margarine

1 tablespoon brown sugar
¼ teaspoon sea salt or to taste

1. Simmer carrots in water until just soft, about 8–10 minutes; do not overcook. Drain and drizzle with lemon juice.
2. Heat together carrots, margarine, brown sugar, and sea salt, stirring frequently until glaze forms and carrots are well coated, about 5 minutes.

Ⓥ Lemon Mint New Potatoes

Serves 6

COST: $0.98
Per ¾ cup
Calories: 221
Fat: 2.5g
Carbohydrates: 45g
Protein: 5g
Fiber: 7g
Sugar: 3g
Sodium: 85mg

10 small new potatoes,
  chopped
4 cloves garlic, minced
1 tablespoon olive oil

¼ cup chopped mint
Salt and pepper to taste
2 teaspoons lemon juice

1. Preheat oven to 350°F. Line or lightly grease a baking sheet.
2. In a large bowl, toss together the potatoes with the garlic, olive oil, and mint, coating potatoes well.
3. Arrange potatoes in a single layer on a baking sheet. Roast for 45 minutes. Season with salt and pepper and drizzle with lemon juice just before serving.

Garlic Bread

Serves 8

COST: $0.25
Per slice
Calories: 230
Fat: 6g
Carbohydrates: 36g
Protein: 7.5g
Fiber: 1.5g
Sugar: 1.5g
Sodium: 416mg

1 loaf Italian bread
3 tablespoons extra-virgin
  olive oil

2 cloves garlic, finely chopped
  (about 1 tablespoon)

1. Preheat oven to 375°F. Laterally split the loaf of bread. Whisk together the olive oil with the chopped garlic.
2. Using a brush or a rubber spatula, generously slather both cut sides of the bread with garlic oil. Place garlic bread halves on a sheet pan or baking dish, and bake in center of oven until crisp and lightly browned, about 20 minutes.
3. Cut each side of the bread into 4 pieces and serve.

Chive Dumplings

Serves 6

COST: $0.77

Per dumpling
Calories: 48
Fat: 1.5g
Carbohydrates: 6g
Protein: 3g
Fiber: 0.5g
Sugar: 1g
Sodium: 209g

1 cup finely diced firm tofu
1 cup finely chopped chives
1 teaspoon sugar
1 teaspoon Asian chili sauce
1 egg white, beaten

1 tablespoon soy sauce
1 teaspoon sesame oil
1 package wonton skins

1. Combine tofu, chives, sugar, chili sauce, all but 1 teaspoon of the egg white, soy sauce, and sesame oil.
2. Place 2 teaspoons of filling onto a wonton skin. Use your finger to moisten the edge of the wonton skin lightly with a bit of the remaining egg white. Fold 2 opposite corners of the skin together to form a triangle shape. Seal edges together by pinching tightly with your fingers. Repeat with remaining filling and wonton wrappers, making as many triangle-shaped dumplings as filling allows. Place them on a plate dusted with cornstarch.
3. Bring 3 quarts water to a rapid boil. Boil the dumplings in batches. Serve with a dumpling sauce.

CHAPTER 6

Whole Grains, Rice, and Pasta

With exams, deadlines, and dating, sometimes you just want to crawl home and indulge in some comfort food. And that's exactly what you'll find in this chapter, which focuses on delicious and satisfying grain-, rice-, and pasta-filled recipes like Vegetarian Lasagna, Quinoa "Mac 'n' Cheese" Casserole, and Easy Fried Rice. Keep in mind though that one-half cup of a cooked whole grain is considered a serving, which is about half your fist. If that doesn't sound like a lot of food, you're not alone. Grain portions have slowly taken over our plate, especially with pasta dishes. Here you'll find dishes that are within serving size. However, it is a good idea to stay between ½ cup (about 100 calories) to 1 cup if you're using the recipe as a side dish. If you're using one of the recipes as a meal, it is safe to have 1–2 cups. Don't worry though, you won't be hungry as long as you put your 1–2 cups of vegetables on your plate first, then your proteins and grains. The good news is that most whole grains are almost complete proteins. With a serving of beans, tofu, nuts, or other plant proteins, you'll have a complete, delicious, nutritious meal that you can brag about in no time.

Whole-Wheat Pasta with Basil and Tomato Pesto

Serves 2

COST: $4.66
Per 1 cup
Calories: 479
Fat: 34g
Carbohydrates: 34g
Protein: 13g
Fiber: 5g
Sugar: 3g
Sodium: 219mg

1 cup rigatoni pasta
1 ounce fresh basil leaves
3 cloves garlic
1 large tomato

¼ cup pine nuts
¼ cup grated Parmesan cheese
⅛ cup olive oil

1. Cook the pasta in boiling salted water until tender but still firm (al dente). Drain. Chop the basil leaves to make 1 cup. Smash, peel, and chop the garlic. Wash and chop the tomato, reserving the juice.
2. Process the garlic and pine nuts in a food processor. One at a time, add and process the tomato and basil leaves. Slowly add the olive oil and keep processing until the pesto is creamy. Add the grated Parmesan cheese. Pour half the pesto sauce over the cooked pasta. Store the remaining pesto sauce in a sealed container in the refrigerator for up to 7 days.

Vegetarian Lasagna

Serves 2

COST: $1.41
Per ½ casserole
Calories: 419
Fat: 9g
Carbohydrates: 60g
Protein: 21g
Fiber: 3g
Sugar: 3g
Sodium: 221mg

½ cup crushed tomatoes
⅓ cup ricotta cheese
⅓ cup grated mozzarella cheese

1 tablespoon grated Parmesan cheese
⅛ teaspoon dried oregano
⅛ teaspoon dried basil
6 oven-ready lasagna noodles

1. Place the crushed tomatoes in a bowl. Stir in the ricotta, then the mozzarella, and then the Parmesan. Make sure each cheese is thoroughly mixed in before adding the next. Stir in the oregano and basil.
2. Lay out 2 lasagna noodles in a large bowl or small (½-quart) microwave-safe casserole dish. Break the noodles in half or as needed to fit the shape of the dish. Spoon approximately ⅓ of the tomato sauce and cheese mixture evenly over the top. Repeat the layering 2 more times.
3. Cover the dish with wax paper. Microwave on high heat for 3 minutes. Turn the bowl, and microwave on high heat for another 3–5 minutes, until the cheese is cooked.

Easy Fried Rice

Serves 2

COST: $2.13

Per ¾ cup
Calories: 236
Fat: 10g
Carbohydrates: 28g
Protein: 7.5g
Fiber: 3.5g
Sugar: 2.5g
Sodium: 38mg

1 large cage-free egg
Salt and pepper, to taste
1 green onion

1 tablespoon coconut oil
1 cup cooked brown rice
½ cup frozen peas

1. Lightly beat the egg with a fork. Stir in the salt and pepper and set aside. Wash the green onion and dice.
2. Heat the vegetable oil in a frying pan over medium-high heat. Add the rice and cook, stirring frequently.
3. Push the rice to the edges of the frying pan. Add the beaten egg in the middle. Use a spatula to scramble the egg. Mix the scrambled egg with the rice.
4. Stir in the frozen peas. Stir in the green onion, and cook for another 2–3 minutes, until heated through. Add more salt, pepper, or other seasonings if desired.

Noodles with Spinach

Serves 2

COST: $1.46

Per 1 cup
Calories: 243
Fat: 16g
Carbohydrates: 19g
Protein: 8g
Fiber: 4g
Sugar: 2g
Sodium: 550mg

1½ cups egg noodles
2 cloves garlic
1 tomato
1 tablespoon olive oil

1 cup thawed frozen spinach
2 tablespoons grated Parmesan cheese
¼ teaspoon sea salt

1. Cook the noodles according to the package instructions. Drain thoroughly.
2. Smash, peel, and chop the garlic cloves. Slice the tomato.
3. Heat the oil in a frying pan over medium heat. Add the garlic and tomato. Cook briefly, turn the heat up to high, and add the noodles.
4. Stir in the spinach. Cook very briefly, mixing the spinach with the noodles, and remove from the heat. Stir in the Parmesan cheese. Season with salt as desired.

Ⓥ Coconut Rice

Serves 4

1 cup water
1 14-ounce coconut milk
1½ cups white rice
⅓ cup coconut flakes
1 teaspoon lime juice
½ teaspoon salt

1. In a large pot, combine the water, coconut milk, and rice and bring to a simmer. Cover and allow to cook 20 minutes, or until rice is done.
2. In a separate skillet, toast the coconut flakes over low heat until lightly golden, about 3 minutes. Gently stir constantly to avoid burning.
3. Combine coconut flakes with cooked rice and stir in lime juice and salt.

Ⓥ Italian Rice Salad

Serves 6

⅓ cup red wine vinegar
1 tablespoon balsamic vinegar
2 teaspoons Dijon mustard
¼ cup olive oil
4 cloves garlic, minced
1 teaspoon basil
⅓ cup chopped fresh parsley
2 cups rice, cooked
1 cup green peas
1 carrot, grated
½ cup roasted red peppers, chopped
½ cup green olives, sliced
Salt and pepper to taste

1. Whisk or shake together the red wine vinegar, balsamic vinegar, Dijon mustard, olive oil, garlic, basil, and parsley.
2. Combine rice with remaining ingredients in a large bowl. Toss with dressing mixture and coat well.
3. Taste, and season with just a bit of salt and pepper.
4. Chill for at least 30 minutes before serving to allow flavors to set, and gently toss again just before serving.

ⓥ Five-Minute Vegan Pasta Salad

Serves 6

COST: $0.98

Per ½ cup
Calories: 276
Fat: 12g
Carbohydrates: 35g
Protein: 7g
Fiber: 5g
Sugar: 3g
Sodium: 427mg

4 cups pasta, cooked
½ cup vegan Italian salad
  dressing
3 scallions, chopped
½ cup sliced black olives

1 tomato, chopped
1 avocado, diced
Salt and pepper to taste

Toss together all ingredients. Allow to chill for at least 1½ hours before serving, if time allows, to allow flavors to combine.

Instant Add-Ons

Open up a jar and instantly add color, flavor, and texture to a basic pasta salad. What's in your cupboard? Try edamame, sunflower seeds, pumpkin seeds, capers, roasted red peppers, jarred pimentos, sun-dried tomatoes, or even mandarin oranges or sliced beets. Snip in any leftover fresh herbs you have on hand.

Ⓥ Basic Tofu Lasagna

Serves 8

COST: $1.38

Per 1 square
Calories: 383
Fat: 6g
Carbohydrates: 52g
Protein: 17g
Fiber: 5g
Sugar: 13g
Sodium: 657mg

1 12-ounce block firm tofu
1 12-ounce block silken tofu
¼ cup nutritional yeast
1 tablespoon lemon juice
1 tablespoon soy sauce (low sodium)
1 teaspoon garlic powder
2 teaspoons basil

3 tablespoons chopped fresh parsley
½ teaspoon salt
4 cups spaghetti sauce (low sodium)
1 16-ounce package lasagna noodles, cooked

1. Preheat oven to 350°F.
2. In a large bowl, mash together the firm tofu, silken tofu, nutritional yeast, lemon juice, soy sauce, garlic powder, basil, parsley, and salt until combined and crumbly like ricotta cheese.
3. To assemble the lasagna, spread about ⅔ cup spaghetti sauce on the bottom of a lasagna pan, then add a layer of noodles.
4. Spread about ½ the tofu mixture on top of the noodles, followed by another layer of sauce. Place a second layer of noodles on top, followed by the remaining tofu and more sauce. Finish it off with a third layer of noodles and the rest of the sauce.
5. Cover and bake for 25 minutes.

Fettuccine Alfredo

Serves 6

8 ounces (½ box) fettuccine
½ cup butter
2 cloves garlic, minced
1 tablespoon flour
1½ cups whole milk
2 tablespoons cream cheese

1 cup grated Parmesan cheese, plus extra for garnish
Salt and freshly ground black pepper

1. Prepare the pasta according to package directions. Drain and keep warm.
2. In a large saucepan, melt the butter; add garlic and cook 2 minutes.
3. Stir in the flour, then add the milk all at once, cooking and stirring over medium heat until thick and bubbly. Add the cream cheese; stir until blended. Add the Parmesan cheese; continue cooking until all cheese has melted. Toss with fettuccine; season with salt and pepper. Serve with extra Parmesan on the side.

Easy Pad Thai Noodles

Serves 6

1 pound thin rice noodles
¼ cup tahini
¼ cup ketchup
¼ cup soy sauce (low sodium)
2 tablespoons rice vinegar
3 tablespoons lime juice
2 tablespoons sugar

¾ teaspoon crushed red pepper flakes
1 block firm tofu, diced small
3 cloves garlic
¼ cup vegetable oil
4 scallions, chopped
½ teaspoon salt

1. Cover the noodles in hot water and set aside to soak until soft, about 5 minutes.
2. Whisk together the tahini, ketchup, soy sauce, vinegar, lime juice, sugar, and red pepper flakes.
3. In a large skillet, fry the tofu and garlic in oil until tofu is lightly golden brown. Add drained noodles, stirring to combine well, and fry for 2–3 minutes.
4. Reduce heat to medium and add tahini mixture, stirring well to combine. Allow to cook for 3–4 minutes until well combined and heated through. Add scallions and salt and heat 1 more minute, stirring well.

Peanut Butter Noodles

Serves 8

COST: $0.75

Per 1 cup serving
Calories: 289
Fat: 7g
Carbohydrates: 50g
Protein: 5g
Fiber: 3g
Sugar: 2g
Sodium: 313mg

1 pound Asian-style noodles
⅓ cup natural peanut butter
⅓ cup water
3 tablespoons soy sauce (low sodium)
2 tablespoons lime juice

2 tablespoons rice vinegar
1 tablespoon sesame oil
½ teaspoon ginger powder
1 teaspoon sugar
½ teaspoon crushed red pepper flakes

Prepare noodles according to package instructions and set aside. Whisk together remaining ingredients over low heat just until combined, about 3 minutes. Toss with noodles.

Asian Sesame Tahini Noodles

Serves 8

COST: $1.15

Per 1 cup
Calories: 315
Fat: 9g
Carbohydrates: 50g
Protein: 5g
Fiber: 3g
Sugar: 1g
Sodium: 295mg

1 pound Asian noodles
½ cup tahini
⅓ cup water
2 tablespoons soy sauce
1 clove garlic
2 teaspoons fresh ginger, minced

2 tablespoons rice vinegar
2 teaspoons sesame oil
1 red bell pepper, sliced thin
3 scallions, chopped
¾ cup snow peas, chopped
¼ teaspoon crushed red pepper flakes

1. Cook noodles according to package instructions; drain well.
2. Whisk or blend together the tahini, water, soy sauce, garlic, ginger, and rice vinegar.
3. In a large skillet, heat the sesame oil, bell pepper, scallions, and snow peas for 2–3 minutes. Add tahini sauce and noodles, stirring well to combine.
4. Cook over low heat just until heated, about 2–3 minutes.
5. Garnish with crushed red pepper flakes to taste.

Lazy and Hungry Garlic Pasta

Serves 3

COST: $0.75

Per 1 cup
Calories: 322
Fat: 10g
Carbohydrates: 45g
Protein: 10g
Fiber: 3g
Sugar: 1g
Sodium: 434mg

2 cloves garlic, minced
2 tablespoons olive oil
3 cups pasta, cooked

2 tablespoons nutritional yeast
½ teaspoon parsley
Salt and pepper to taste

Heat the garlic in olive oil for 1–2 minutes, or until almost browned. Toss garlic and olive oil with remaining ingredients. Adjust seasonings to taste.

Really Hungry? Really Lazy?

Garlic powder, nutritional yeast, and salt is a delicious seasoning combination that will give a B_{12} boost to your energy levels and mood. Use it over toast, veggies, popcorn, bagels, baked potatoes, and, of course, cooked pasta.

California Picnic Pasta Salad

Serves 6

COST: $0.75

Per 1 cup
Calories: 290
Fat: 16g
Carbohydrates: 32g
Protein: 7g
Fiber: 7g
Sugar: 3g
Sodium: 316mg

3 cups bow-tie pasta, cooked
2 large tomatoes, diced
½ cup jarred banana peppers, sliced thin
½ red onion, diced
½ cup sliced black olives
2 tablespoons olive oil

1 tablespoon lemon juice
2 teaspoons Dijon mustard
1 tablespoon red wine vinegar
½ teaspoon basil
½ teaspoon oregano
Salt and pepper to taste
2 avocados, diced

1. Combine the pasta, tomatoes, peppers, onion, and olives in a large bowl. In a separate small bowl, whisk together the remaining ingredients, except avocado, until well mixed.
2. Chill for at least 1 hour.
3. Add diced avocado and toss gently. Serve immediately.

Homemade Garlic and Herb Gnocchi

Serves 4

COST: $0.42

Per 8 gnocchi
Calories: 281
Fat: 1g
Carbohydrates: 58g
Protein: 7g
Fiber: 3g
Sugar: 7g
Sodium: 443mg

2 large potatoes
¾ teaspoon garlic powder
½ teaspoon dried basil
½ teaspoon dried parsley
¾ teaspoon salt
1½ cups all-purpose flour
4 cups water for boiling

1. Bake potatoes until done, about 50 minutes at 400°F. Allow to cool, then peel skins.
2. Using a fork, mash potatoes with garlic powder, basil, parsley, and salt until potatoes are completely smooth, with no lumps.
3. On a floured work surface, place half of the flour, then add the potatoes on top. Use your hands to work the flour into the potatoes to form a dough. Continue to add only as much flour as is needed to form a dough. Knead smooth.
4. Working in batches, roll out a rope of dough about 1 inch thick. Slice into 1-inch-long pieces, and gently roll against a fork to make grooves in the dough. This helps the sauce stick to the dough.
5. Cook gnocchi in boiling water for 2–3 minutes until they rise to the surface. Serve immediately.

Zucchini and Fresh Basil Pomodoro

Serves 4

COST: $3.75

Per 1 cup
Calories: 224
Fat: 8g
Carbohydrates: 32g
Protein: 7g
Fiber: 4.5g
Sugar: 7g
Sodium: 18mg

2 zucchini, sliced
4 cloves garlic, minced
2 tablespoons olive oil
4 large tomatoes, diced
⅓ cup chopped fresh basil

2 cups prepared angel hair pasta
Salt and pepper to taste

1. Heat zucchini and garlic over low heat in olive oil for 1–2 minutes, or until zucchini is just lightly softened. Add tomatoes and cook for another 4–5 minutes.
2. Toss zucchini and tomatoes with basil and pasta and season with salt and pepper, to taste.

Mexican Rice

Serves 6

COST: $0.79

Per ¾ cup
Calories: 310
Fat: 12g
Carbohydrates: 44g
Protein: 4g
Fiber: 3g
Sugar: 3g
Sodium: 524mg

1½ cups long-grain white rice
1 large tomato, peeled, seeded, and chopped
⅓ medium white onion, roughly chopped
1 clove garlic, peeled and roughly chopped

⅓ cup safflower oil
3½ cups vegetable stock
2 teaspoons salt
½ carrot, peeled and finely chopped
⅓ cup frozen green peas

1. Soak rice in hot water for 15 minutes; rinse and drain. Purée the tomato, onion, and garlic in a blender.
2. In a large saucepot over medium heat, fry the rice in the oil until it turns light gold in color, about 10 minutes. Pour off excess oil. Stir in the tomato purée and cook until almost dry, about 3 minutes.
3. Add stock, salt, carrots, and peas. Cover, and simmer over low heat for 18 minutes; liquid should be absorbed and rice tender. Remove from heat and let stand 5 minutes, then fluff with a fork.

Easy Vegetable Risotto

Serves 8

COST: $0.89
Per ¾ cup
Calories: 384
Fat: 10g
Carbohydrates: 56g
Protein: 12g
Fiber: 4g
Sugar: 2g
Sodium: 658mg

10 cups vegetable stock
2 tablespoons olive oil
1 onion, roughly chopped
1 pound short-grain Italian rice
    for risotto, such as arborio
½ cup dry white wine

1½ cups grated Parmesan
    cheese
1 pound frozen mixed
    vegetables
Salt and freshly ground black
    pepper to taste
1 tablespoon unsalted butter

1. Heat the stock until hot but not boiling. Heat the oil separately in a heavy-bottomed saucepan over medium heat; add the onion and cook until translucent, about 5 minutes. Stir in the rice and mix with a wooden spoon until rice is well coated and begins to change color, about 5 minutes.
2. Add the white wine; cook until all wine is absorbed. Begin adding the hot stock in 1-cup increments, stirring each time until all the liquid is absorbed before adding the next cup, until rice is soft and creamy and you have only 1 cup of liquid left.
3. Fold in the cheese, vegetables, salt, pepper, and butter. Stir until well combined; remove from heat. Adjust consistency with remaining stock. Rice should have a saucy consistency and be soft, but still have a little bite (al dente).

Fried Rice with Green Peas and Egg

Serves 4

COST: $0.67

Per 1½ cups
Calories: 427
Fat: 11g
Carbohydrates: 67g
Protein: 13g
Fiber: 4g
Sugar: 4g
Sodium: 131mg

2 tablespoons peanut oil
3 eggs, beaten
2 tablespoons chopped ginger
2 tablespoons chopped garlic
½ cup chopped scallions

4 cups cooked white rice
1 10-ounce package frozen
    green peas
1 tablespoon soy sauce

1. Heat a 10-inch nonstick skillet with a few drops of oil over medium heat; add the eggs. Cook without stirring until completely cooked through, about 3 minutes. Slide the cooked egg sheet onto a cutting board; let it cool for 5 minutes. Roll the egg into a cylinder, and crosscut to form long julienne.
2. Heat the oil in a large skillet or wok. Add the ginger, garlic, and scallions, and cook for 1 minute; they should sizzle. Add the rice. Over high heat, chop and stir the rice to break up any lumps; cook until very hot, and rice forms crunchy bits, about 5 minutes. Add the peas, cook until hot, then stir in the egg julienne, and soy sauce. Serve garnished with additional chopped scallions.

Ⓥ Wild Rice with Apples and Almonds

Serves 4

COST: $1.54

Per ¾ cup
Calories: 261
Fat: 13g
Carbohydrates: 33g
Protein: 7g
Fiber: 4g
Sugar: 11g
Sodium: 4mg

½ cup wild rice
½ cup shelled almonds, whole
    or in slivers
1 tablespoon oil
1 large onion, roughly chopped
1 apple, peeled, cored, and
    diced

¼ cup raisins
Salt and freshly ground black
    pepper to taste
1 tablespoon olive oil
¼ cup chopped parsley

1. Boil the rice in 2½ quarts salted water until tender, about 40 minutes; drain, saving cooking liquid. Toast the almonds dry (no oil) in a skillet over medium heat until visibly shiny, about 5 minutes.
2. Heat the oil in a large skillet over medium heat for 1 minute. Add onions; cook until softened, about 5 minutes. Add the apple, raisins, and a splash of the rice cooking liquid. Cook 5 minutes more, until the apples are translucent.
3. Combine the cooked rice, the apple mixture, the almonds, and salt and pepper. Stir in olive oil, if desired, and serve garnished with parsley.

Ⓥ Pineapple Lime Rice

Serves 4

COST: $1.19
Per ¾ cup
Calories: 240
Fat: 6g
Carbohydrates: 44g
Protein: 3g
Fiber: 2g
Sugar: 16g
Sodium: 68mg

2 tablespoons vegan margarine
2 cups rice, cooked
1½ tablespoons lime juice
⅓ cup chopped fresh cilantro

1 16-ounce can pineapple tid-
  bits, drained
Dash sea salt

Stir vegan margarine into hot rice until melted and combined. Add remaining ingredients, tossing gently to combine. Taste, and add a dash of salt, to taste.

Wild Rice Vegetable Pancakes

Serves 6

COST: $0.53
Per 1 pancake
Calories: 113
Fat: 1.5g
Carbohydrates: 20g
Protein: 5g
Fiber: 2g
Sugar: 2g
Sodium: 41mg

4 ounces wild rice
1 cup julienne carrots
1 cup julienne celery
1 cup julienne white onion
3 scallions, chopped

2 eggs
½ cup flour
Kosher salt and freshly ground
  black pepper
Olive oil for frying

1. Boil the wild rice in 2 quarts lightly salted water until very tender and most grains have burst open, about 40 minutes. Drain, reserving liquid, and cool the rice by spreading it on a platter or pan. Toss the rice with the carrots, celery, onion, scallions, eggs, and flour. Season with salt and pepper. Moisten with a few drips of rice-cooking liquid to help the mixture adhere to itself.
2. Heat 2 tablespoons olive oil in a nonstick skillet over medium heat until a piece of onion sizzles when added, about 2 minutes. Place quarter-cup mounds of rice mixture into the pan; shape them into rough-hewn pancakes. Cook without moving them until they brown on the first side and are visibly cooked around the edges, about 5 minutes. Flip the pancakes with a spatula, and cook until lightly browned. Drain. Serve.

Linguine with Olives, Capers, and Tomatoes

Serves 8

COST: $0.97

Per ¾ cup
Calories: 273
Fat: 5g
Carbohydrates: 48g
Protein: 9g
Fiber: 4g
Sugar: 5g
Sodium: 434mg

2 tablespoons olive oil
1 tablespoon chopped garlic
½ cup kalamata olives, pitted
1 tablespoon small (nonpareil) capers
Pinch of crushed red pepper flakes

½ cup roughly chopped Italian parsley
2 cups chopped tomatoes
2 cups tomato sauce
Salt and pepper to taste
1 pound linguine, cooked al dente, drained, rinsed, and tossed with olive oil

1. Heat the olive oil and garlic in a large, heavy-bottomed skillet or Dutch oven until it sizzles; add the olives, capers, red pepper flakes, and parsley. Cook 2 minutes; add the tomatoes. Cook until the tomatoes soften into a chunky sauce; add the tomato sauce, season to taste, and bring back to a simmer.
2. Add the cooked linguine; cook until heated through. Remove from heat, adjust seasoning. Serve sprinkled with additional chopped parsley.

Ⓥ Farfalle (Bow-Ties) Fra Diavolo

Serves 8

COST: $1.97

Per ¾ cup
Calories: 327
Fat: 7g
Carbohydrates: 56g
Protein: 9g
Fiber: 4g
Sugar: 7g
Sodium: 409mg

2 tablespoons olive oil
1 tablespoon finely chopped garlic (about 3 cloves)
½ teaspoon crushed red pepper flakes
1 cup roughly chopped Italian parsley

1 28-ounce jar store-bought tomato sauce
1 pound farfalle, cooked al dente
Kosher salt and freshly ground black pepper

1. Bring a pot of water to a boil for reheating the pasta. Heat a large skillet or heavy-bottomed pot large enough to hold all the ingredients over high heat. Add the oil, garlic, pepper flakes, and parsley; allow these ingredients to sizzle for 30 seconds. Add the tomato sauce; bring to a simmer.
2. Using a colander or China cap (a funnel-shaped strainer), dip the cooked pasta into the boiling water for 1 minute to reheat. Transfer the reheated pasta into the sauce, letting the water that adheres to the pasta drip into the sauce and thin it a little. Toss to coat; adjust consistency with additional pasta water, and season with salt and pepper to taste. Serve sprinkled with additional chopped parsley.

Ⓥ Baked Mexican Rice Casserole

Serves 4

COST: $0.71

Per 1 cup
Calories: 248
Fat: 1g
Carbohydrates: 50g
Protein: 9g
Fiber: 7g
Sugar: 4g
Sodium: 616mg

1 15-ounce can black beans
¾ cup salsa
2 teaspoons chili powder
1 teaspoon cumin

½ cup corn kernels
2 cups rice, cooked
½ cup grated vegan cheese
⅓ cup sliced black olives

1. Preheat oven to 350°F.
2. Combine the beans, salsa, chili powder, and cumin in a large pot over low heat; partially mash beans with a large fork.
3. Remove from heat and stir in corn and rice. Transfer to a casserole dish.
4. Top with vegan cheese and sliced olives and bake for 20 minutes.

Ⓥ Italian White Beans and Rice

Serves 4

COST: $1.59

Per 1 cup
Calories: 248
Fat: 8g
Carbohydrates: 35g
Protein: 12g
Fiber: 8g
Sugar: 5g
Sodium: 135mg

½ onion, diced
2 ribs celery, diced
3 cloves garlic, minced
2 tablespoons olive oil
1 12-ounce can crushed
   tomatoes

1 15-ounce can cannellini
   beans, drained
½ teaspoon parsley
½ teaspoon basil
1 cup rice, cooked
1 tablespoon balsamic vinegar

1. Sauté onion, celery, and garlic in olive oil for 3–5 minutes until onion and celery are soft.
2. Reduce heat to medium low and add tomatoes, beans, parsley, and basil. Cover and simmer for 10 minutes, stirring occasionally.
3. Stir in cooked rice and balsamic vinegar and cook, uncovered, for a few more minutes until liquid is absorbed.

Green Rice Pilaf

Serves 6

COST: $0.59

Per ¾ cup
Calories: 306
Fat: 6g
Carbohydrates: 56g
Protein: 5g
Fiber: 2g
Sugar: 3g
Sodium: 375mg

3 tablespoons butter
2 cups chopped onion
2 cups long-grain rice
½ cup (packed) mixed chopped herbs (chives, parsley, and dill)
4 cups vegetable stock
Salt and pepper to taste
1 bay leaf

1. In a medium saucepan, melt the butter over a medium flame. Add the onion; cook until translucent, about 5 minutes. Add the rice; cook, stirring often, until the rice is well coated and becomes golden.
2. In a blender, combine the herbs, stock, salt, and pepper; blend until herbs are finely chopped. Add to the rice; bring to a boil, add the bay leaf, and then lower to a very slow simmer. Cover tightly; cook until rice has absorbed all liquid, about 25 minutes. Fluff with a fork, then cover and let stand for 5 minutes before serving. Remove bay leaf before serving.

Ⓥ Cuban Black Beans, Sweet Potatoes, and Rice

Serves 4

COST: $1.87

Per 1 cup
Calories: 387
Fat: 8g
Carbohydrates: 76g
Protein: 13g
Fiber: 13g
Sugar: 8g
Sodium: 491mg

3 cloves garlic, minced
2 large sweet potatoes, chopped small
2 tablespoons olive oil
2 15-ounce cans black beans, drained
¾ cup vegetable broth
1 tablespoon chili powder
1 teaspoon paprika
1 teaspoon cumin
1 tablespoon lime juice
Hot sauce, to taste
2 cups rice, cooked

1. In a large skillet or pot, sauté garlic and sweet potatoes in olive oil for 2–3 minutes.
2. Reduce heat to medium low and add beans, vegetable broth, chili powder, paprika, and cumin. Bring to a simmer, cover, and allow to cook for 25–30 minutes until sweet potatoes are soft.
3. Stir in lime juice and hot sauce, to taste. Serve hot over rice.

Ⓥ Quinoa and Chutney Salad

Serves 6

COST: $1.06
Per ⅓ cup
Calories: 188
Fat: 4g
Carbohydrates: 35g
Protein: 4g
Fiber: 2g
Sugar: 11g
Sodium: 110mg

1 cup quinoa, boiled for 15 minutes, drained
1 cup store-bought tomato chutney
¼ teaspoon kosher salt
1 tablespoon extra-virgin olive oil

Combine the cooked quinoa and tomato chutney. Season to taste. Dress with olive oil, and serve with extra olive oil at the table.

Ⓥ Lemon Quinoa Veggie Salad

Serves 4

COST: $1.79
Per 1 cup
Calories: 379
Fat: 17g
Carbohydrates: 49g
Protein: 10g
Fiber: 5.5g
Sugar: 2.5g
Sodium: 856mg

4 cups vegetable broth
1½ cups quinoa
1 cup frozen mixed veggies, thawed
¼ cup lemon juice
¼ cup olive oil
1 teaspoon garlic powder
½ teaspoon sea salt
¼ teaspoon black pepper
2 tablespoons chopped fresh parsley

1. In a large pot, bring vegetable broth to a boil. Add quinoa, cover, and simmer for 15–20 minutes, stirring occasionally, until liquid is absorbed and quinoa is cooked. Add mixed veggies and stir to combine.
2. Remove from heat and combine with remaining ingredients. Serve hot or cold.

Ⓥ Easy Garlic Quinoa

Serves 4

COST: $0.79

Per ¾ cup
Calories: 339
Fat: 10g
Carbohydrates: 48g
Protein: 10g
Fiber: 5.5g
Sugar: 2.5g
Sodium: 656mg

1 yellow onion, diced
4 cloves garlic, minced
2 tablespoons olive oil
3 cups vegetable broth

1½ cups quinoa
½ teaspoon salt
3 tablespoons nutritional yeast

1. In a large skillet, heat onion and garlic in oil or margarine for 3–4 minutes until onions are soft.
2. Add vegetable broth and quinoa, cover, and bring to a simmer. Allow to cook for 15 minutes until liquid is absorbed.
3. Fluff quinoa with a fork and stir in salt and nutritional yeast.

Ⓥ Couscous and Bean Pilaf

Serves 4

COST: $1.39

Per 1½ cups
Calories: 476
Fat: 8g
Carbohydrates: 82g
Protein: 16g
Fiber: 10g
Sugar: 2g
Sodium: 324mg

2 cups water or vegetable broth
2 cups couscous
2 tablespoons olive oil
2 tablespoons red wine vinegar
½ teaspoon crushed red pepper flakes

1 15-ounce can cannellini beans, drained
2 tablespoons minced pimiento peppers
2 tablespoons chopped fresh parsley
Salt and pepper to taste

1. Bring the water or vegetable broth to a simmer and add couscous. Cover, turn off heat, and allow to sit for at least 15 minutes to cook couscous. Fluff with a fork.
2. Whisk together the olive oil, red wine vinegar, and red pepper flakes and toss with cooked couscous.
3. Combine beans, pimiento peppers, and parsley with couscous, tossing gently to combine. Season generously with salt and pepper.

Whole Grains, Rice, and Pasta   151

Ⓥ Quinoa "Mac 'n' Cheese" Casserole

Serves 6

COST: $1.89

Per 1 cup
Calories: 367
Fat: 14g
Carbohydrates: 40g
Protein: 15g
Fiber: 6g
Sugar: 4g
Sodium: 624mg

1½ cups quinoa
3 cups vegetable broth
1 onion, chopped
3 cloves garlic, minced
2 tablespoons olive oil
1 bunch broccoli, diced small
1 large tomato, diced

1 tablespoon flour
¾ cup soy milk
½ teaspoon sea salt
1 cup shredded vegan cheese
½ teaspoon dried parsley
1 cup seasoned bread crumbs
¼ teaspoon nutmeg

1. Preheat oven to 350°F.
2. Simmer quinoa in vegetable broth, covered, until done and liquid is absorbed, about 15 minutes.
3. In a medium skillet or saucepan, heat onion and garlic in olive oil and add broccoli and tomato. Heat, stirring frequently, for 3–4 minutes.
4. Add flour, stirring to coat well, then add soy milk and sea salt, stirring until thick, about 3 minutes.
5. Combine quinoa, broccoli-and-soy-milk mixture, and half the vegan cheese in a large casserole. Sprinkle the other half of the cheese on top, along with parsley and bread crumbs and nutmeg.
6. Bake for 10–12 minutes, or until cheese is melted.

Ⓥ Mediterranean Quinoa Pilaf

Serves 4

COST: $1.60

Per ¾ cup
Calories: 360
Fat: 12g
Carbohydrates: 52g
Protein: 10g
Fiber: 7g
Sugar: 6g
Sodium: 324mg

1½ cups quinoa
3 cups vegetable broth
3 tablespoons balsamic
   vinegar
2 tablespoons olive oil
1 tablespoon lemon juice
⅓ teaspoon salt

½ cup sun-dried tomatoes,
   chopped
½ cup artichoke hearts,
   chopped
½ cup kalamata olives, sliced

1. In a large skillet or saucepan, bring the quinoa and vegetable broth to a boil, then reduce to a simmer. Cover, and allow quinoa to cook until liquid is absorbed, about 15 minutes. Remove from heat, fluff quinoa with a fork, and allow to stand another 5 minutes.
2. Stir in the balsamic vinegar, olive oil, lemon juice, and salt, then add remaining ingredients, gently tossing to combine. Serve hot.

Ⓥ Barley and Mushroom Pilaf

Serves 4

COST: $1.23

Per ¾ cup
Calories: 331
Fat: 9g
Carbohydrates: 56g
Protein: 8g
Fiber: 11g
Sugar: 3g
Sodium: 339mg

1 cup sliced porcini
   mushrooms
1 cup sliced shiitake
   mushrooms
2 ribs celery, diced
½ onion, chopped
3 tablespoons olive oil, divided

1¼ cups barley
3¾ cups vegetable broth
1 bay leaf
¼ teaspoon sage
½ teaspoon parsley
½ teaspoon thyme

1. In a large skillet or stock pot, sauté mushrooms, celery, and onion in 2 tablespoons olive oil until almost soft, about 2–3 minutes. Add barley and remaining 1 tablespoon olive oil and allow to toast for 1–2 minutes, stirring frequently.
2. When barley starts to turn brown, add vegetable broth and seasonings. Bring to a simmer, cover, and allow to cook for 20–25 minutes, stirring occasionally, until liquid is absorbed and barley is cooked. Remove bay leaf before serving.

Ⓥ Barley Baked Beans

Serves 8

COST: $0.67

Per ½ cup
Calories: 224
Fat: 1g
Carbohydrates: 56g
Protein: 8g
Fiber: 9g
Sugar: 3g
Sodium: 849mg

2 cups cooked barley
2 15-ounce cans pinto beans, drained
1 onion, diced
1 28-ounce can crushed tomatoes
½ cup water

¼ cup brown sugar
⅓ cup barbecue sauce
2 tablespoons molasses
2 teaspoons mustard powder
1 teaspoon garlic powder
1 teaspoon salt

1. Preheat oven to 300°F.
2. Combine all ingredients in a large casserole or baking dish. Cover, and bake for 2 hours, stirring occasionally.
3. Uncover and bake for 15 more minutes or until thick and saucy.

Ⓥ Bulgur Wheat Tabbouleh Salad with Tomatoes

Serves 4

COST: $3.99

Per ½ cup
Calories: 250
Fat: 11g
Carbohydrates: 35g
Protein: 7g
Fiber: 10g
Sugar: 4.5g
Sodium: 315mg

1¼ cups boiling water
1 cup bulgur wheat
3 tablespoons olive oil
¼ cup lemon juice
1 teaspoon garlic powder
½ teaspoon sea salt

½ teaspoon pepper
3 scallions, chopped
½ cup chopped fresh mint
½ cup chopped fresh parsley
3 large tomatoes, diced

1. Pour boiling water over bulgur wheat. Cover, and allow to sit for 30 minutes, or until bulgur wheat is soft.
2. Toss bulgur wheat with olive oil, lemon juice, garlic powder, and salt, stirring well to coat. Combine with remaining ingredients, adding in tomatoes last.
3. Allow to chill for at least 1 hour before serving.

Ⓥ Egyptian Lentils and Rice

Serves 4

COST: $0.79

Per ¾ cup
Calories: 303
Fat: 4g
Carbohydrates: 56g
Protein: 9.5g
Fiber: 4.5g
Sugar: 1g
Sodium: 298mg

1 tablespoon olive oil
¼ teaspoon cumin seeds
1 medium onion, roughly
  chopped
1 cup rice

½ cup lentils
2 teaspoons juice plus ½ teaspoon zest from a lemon
1 teaspoon salt
3 cups vegetable stock

1. Heat the oil and cumin seeds in a medium saucepan over medium heat until the seeds are fragrant, about 30 seconds.
2. Add the onion; cook until translucent, about 5 minutes. Stir in the rice and lentils, mixing with a wooden spoon until well coated. Add the lemon juice, zest, salt, and stock.
3. Cover tightly and simmer until all water is absorbed, about 20 minutes. Remove from heat and allow to stand for 5 minutes before fluffing with a fork and serving. Goes great with a dab of Egyptian chili sauce (harissa) or other chili paste.

Polenta with Butter and Cheese

Serves 4

COST: $0.49

Per ½ cup
Calories: 206
Fat: 7g
Carbohydrates: 27g
Protein: 7g
Fiber: 1g
Sugar: 0.5g
Sodium: 495mg

4 cups water, boiling
1 teaspoon salt
1 cup coarse yellow cornmeal
  (polenta)

½ cup grated Parmesan
  cheese
1 tablespoon butter

1. Add salt to the boiling water. Whisking constantly with a stiff wire whisk, gradually pour cornmeal into water in a steady stream, whisking out lumps. Continue whisking constantly until mixture thickens.
2. Lower heat to a very low simmer. You should see only the occasional bubble plopping up through the polenta. Beware: The polenta is molten lava at this point, and spattering can be hazardous. Stir regularly with a wooden spoon until full thickening is achieved, about 25 minutes. Stir in cheese and butter; remove from heat. Serve immediately, or allow to cool for grilling or frying.

Ⓥ Lemon Cilantro Couscous

Serves 4

COST: $0.39
Per ½ cup
Calories: 168
Fat: 0g
Carbohydrates: 35g
Protein: 5.5g
Fiber: 2g
Sugar: 1g
Sodium: 427mg

2 cups vegetable broth
1 cup couscous
⅓ cup lemon juice

½ cup chopped fresh cilantro
¼ teaspoon sea salt, or to taste

1. Bring vegetable broth to a simmer and add couscous. Cover and let stand for 10 minutes, until soft, then fluff with a fork.
2. Stir in lemon juice and cilantro, and season generously with sea salt.

Ⓥ Orange and Raisin Curried Couscous

Serves 6

COST: $1.09
Per ¾ cup
Calories: 345
Fat: 10g
Carbohydrates: 55g
Protein: 9g
Fiber: 5g
Sugar: 13g
Sodium: 8.5mg

2 cups water or vegetable broth
1½ cups couscous
½ cup orange juice
1 onion, chopped
2 tablespoons olive oil

½ teaspoon coriander powder
1 teaspoon curry powder
2 scallions, chopped
¾ cup golden raisins
¾ cup pine nuts

1. Bring water or vegetable broth to a boil. Add couscous and remove from heat. Stir in orange juice, cover, and allow to sit for 15 minutes until most of the liquid is absorbed and couscous is soft.
2. Heat onion in olive oil for 1–2 minutes, then add spices and heat for 1 more minute until fragrant.
3. Combine couscous with spices, and add scallions, raisins, and nuts.

Ⓥ Bell Peppers Stuffed with Couscous

Serves 8

COST: $1.09
Per 1 pepper
Calories: 314
Fat: 4g
Carbohydrates: 48g
Protein: 10g
Fiber: 6g
Sugar: 4g
Sodium: 16mg

4 cups vegetable broth
3 cups couscous
2 tablespoons olive oil
2 tablespoons lemon juice
1 cup frozen peas, thawed

2 green onions, sliced
½ teaspoon cumin
½ teaspoon chili powder
8 green bell peppers

1. Preheat oven to 350°F.
2. Bring vegetable broth to a boil and add couscous. Cover, turn off heat, and let sit for 10–15 minutes until couscous is cooked. Fluff with a fork.
3. Combine couscous with olive oil, lemon juice, peas, green onions, cumin, and chili powder.
4. Cut the tops off the bell peppers and remove seeds.
5. Stuff couscous into bell peppers and place the tops back on, using a toothpick to secure if needed.
6. Transfer to a baking dish and bake for 15 minutes.

Baked Millet Patties

Yields 8 patties

COST: $1.52
Per 1 patty
Calories: 182
Fat: 9g
Carbohydrates: 20g
Protein: 6g
Fiber: 3g
Sugar: 1g
Sodium: 116mg

1½ cups cooked millet
½ cup tahini
1 cup bread crumbs
1 teaspoon parsley

¾ teaspoon garlic powder
½ teaspoon onion powder
⅓ teaspoon salt

1. Preheat oven to 350°F.
2. Combine all ingredients together in a bowl, mashing to mix well.
3. Use your hands to press firmly into patties, about 1 inch thick, and place on a baking sheet.
4. Bake for 10–12 minutes on each side. Then, serve with your favorite side of vegetables for a complete meal.

CHAPTER 7

Main Courses

They say that breakfast is the most important meal of the day and that you need to eat lunch and snacks throughout the day to keep you energized and awake for those late-afternoon classes. But dinner is also important, and with delicious recipes like Easy Eggplant Parmigiana, Black Bean and Butternut Squash Chili, and Portobello and Pepper Fajitas, it may just be your favorite meal of the day! Keep in mind that following a healthy, vegetarian diet doesn't have to mean cooking every night, either! Many of the recipes found in this chapter provide several servings that can be put into individual containers and stored in the refrigerator or freezer for future meals. Delicious and easy? Looks like it's time to start making dinner!

Three-Bean Cassoulet

Serves 2

1 clove garlic
4 ounces fresh snap beans
1 zucchini
⅓ cup chopped white onion
1 cup Romano beans (also
  called Italian flat beans)

¾ cup black-eyed peas
1 cup tomato sauce
1 cup vegetable broth
1 teaspoon dried parsley flakes
½ teaspoon dried basil
⅛ teaspoon (or to taste) salt

1. Preheat oven to 350°F.
2. Smash, peel, and chop the garlic clove. Wash the snap beans and drain. Trim the ends and cut off any brown spots. Wash, peel, and slice the zucchini.
3. Bring a pot of water to a boil. Blanch the snap beans in the boiling water for about 3 minutes, until they turn bright green.
4. Combine the garlic, snap beans, zucchini, onion, Romano beans, black-eyed peas, tomato sauce, and chicken broth in an ungreased 1½- or 2-quart casserole dish.
5. Stir in the dried parsley, dried basil, and the salt.
6. Bake for 2–2½ hours, stirring occasionally, until the vegetables are tender and the cassoulet has thickened.

Vegetarian Cabbage Rolls

Yields 10 cabbage rolls

COST: $2.17
5 rolls (serves 2)
Calories: 186
Fat: 7g
Carbohydrates: 23g
Protein: 9g
Fiber: 5g
Sugar: 15g
Sodium: 493mg

6 ounces firm tofu
2 teaspoons olive oil
1 clove garlic, minced
½ red onion, chopped
1 cup crushed tomatoes
½ green bell pepper
½ teaspoon ground cumin

⅛ teaspoon (or to taste) paprika
10 boiled cabbage leaves
6 ounces tomato sauce
3 ounces water
2 tablespoons white vinegar
2 teaspoons granulated sugar

1. Preheat oven to 350°F. Spray a large baking sheet with nonstick cooking spray.
2. Drain the tofu and dice into small pieces. Heat the olive oil in a medium-sized frying pan. Add the garlic and red onion. Sauté until the onion is tender. Crumble the tofu into the frying pan. Add the tomatoes and green pepper, mashing the tomatoes with a spatula to break them up slightly. Stir in the ground cumin and paprika.
3. Lay a cabbage leaf flat on the counter. Spread 2 heaping tablespoons of filling in the middle (the exact amount needed will depend on the size of the cabbage leaf). Roll up the bottom, tuck in the sides, and continue rolling up to the top. Place the roll in the baking dish, with the seamed section on the bottom.
4. In a small bowl, mix together the tomato sauce, water, white vinegar, and sugar. Pour over the cabbage rolls. Place the dish in the oven and bake the cabbage rolls for 40–45 minutes.

Freezing Cabbage Rolls

Frozen cabbage rolls reheat very nicely, making a quick and easy dinner for busy weeknights. Allow the cooked cabbage rolls to cool and place in resealable plastic freezer bags with a small amount of tomato sauce. Thaw before reheating.

Sesame Baked Tofu

Serves 6

COST: $0.51

Per 4-oz. serving
Calories: 93
Fat: 6g
Carbohydrates: 3g
Protein: 8g
Fiber: 1g
Sugar: 1g
Sodium: 418mg

¼ cup soy sauce (low sodium)
2 tablespoons sesame oil
¾ teaspoon garlic powder

½ teaspoon ginger powder
2 blocks extra-firm tofu, well
  pressed

1. Whisk together the soy sauce, sesame oil, garlic, and ginger powder and transfer to a wide, shallow pan. Slice the tofu into ½-inch-thick strips or triangles. Place the tofu in a plastic bag, pour the marinade in, seal, and set in the fridge. Allow to marinate for at least 1 hour or overnight.
2. Preheat oven to 400°F. Coat a baking sheet well with nonstick spray or olive oil, or line with foil. Place tofu on sheet.
3. Bake for 20–25 minutes, turn over, then bake for another 10–15 minutes or until done.

Marinating Tofu

For marinated baked tofu dishes, a zipper-top bag can be helpful in getting the tofu well covered with marinade. Place the tofu in the bag, pour the marinade in, seal, and set in the fridge, turning and lightly shaking occasionally to coat all sides of the tofu.

Easy Fried Tofu

Serves 3

COST: $2.17

Per ¾ cup
Calories: 132
Fat: 10g
Carbohydrates: 8g
Protein: 9g
Fiber: 2g
Sugar: 15g
Sodium: 208mg

1 block extra-firm tofu, cubed
¼ cup soy sauce
2 tablespoons flour
2 tablespoons nutritional yeast

1 teaspoon garlic powder
¼ teaspoon salt
Dash pepper
¼ cup oil for frying

1. Marinate sliced tofu in soy sauce for at least 1 hour.
2. In a small bowl, combine flour, nutritional yeast, garlic powder, salt, and pepper.
3. Coat tofu well with flour mixture on all sides, then fry in hot oil until crispy and lightly golden brown on all sides, about 4–5 minutes.

Ⓥ Lemon Basil Tofu

Serves 6

COST: $1.28

Per 3 slices or 4 oz.
of tofu
Calories: 130
Fat: 7g
Carbohydrates: 11g
Protein: 10g
Fiber: 6g
Sugar: 1.5g
Sodium: 398mg

3 tablespoons lemon juice
1 tablespoon soy sauce
2 teaspoons apple cider
vinegar
1 tablespoon Dijon mustard
¾ teaspoon sugar

3 tablespoons olive oil
2 tablespoons chopped basil,
plus extra for garnish
2 blocks extra-firm tofu, well
pressed

1. Whisk together all ingredients, except tofu, and transfer to a baking dish or casserole pan.
2. Slice the tofu into ½-inch-thick strips or triangles. Place the tofu in the marinade and coat well. Allow to marinate for at least 1 hour or overnight, being sure tofu is well coated in marinade.
3. Preheat oven to 350°F. Bake for 15 minutes, turn over, then bake for another 10–12 minutes or until done. Garnish with a few extra bits of chopped fresh basil.

Tofu Sticks

Serves 3

COST: $0.92

Per 4 sticks
Calories: 258
Fat: 4.5g
Carbohydrates: 38g
Protein: 15g
Fiber: 3g
Sugar: 3g
Sodium: 354mg

¼ cup flour
⅓ cup soy milk
2 tablespoons lemon juice
1 cup finely ground bread
 crumbs
2 tablespoons dulse seaweed
 flakes

1 tablespoon Old Bay seasoning blend
1 teaspoon onion powder
1 block extra-firm tofu, well
 pressed

1. Preheat oven to 350°F.
2. Place flour in a shallow bowl or pie tin and set aside. Combine the soy milk and lemon juice in a separate shallow bowl or pie tin. In a third bowl or pie tin, combine the bread crumbs, kelp, Old Bay, and onion powder.
3. Slice tofu into 12 ½-inch-thick strips. Place each strip into the flour mixture to coat well, then dip into the soy milk. Next, place each strip into the bread crumbs, gently patting to coat well.
4. Bake for 15–20 minutes, turn once, then bake for another 10–15 minutes or until crispy. Serve with ketchup or a vegan tartar sauce and vegetables.

Tartar Sauce

To make a simple vegan tartar sauce, combine vegan mayonnaise with sweet pickle relish and a generous squeeze of lemon juice. Or dip your fishy tofu sticks in ketchup or barbecue sauce.

Easy Eggplant Parmigiana

Serves 4

COST: $2.03
Per ¼ recipe
Calories: 173
Fat: 9g
Carbohydrates: 11g
Protein: 11g
Fiber: 3g
Sugar: 6g
Sodium: 573mg

1 medium eggplant
½ teaspoon dried basil
½ teaspoon dried oregano
⅛ teaspoon (or to taste) garlic salt
1 cup spaghetti sauce

4 slices mozzarella cheese
¼ cup grated Parmesan cheese

1. Preheat oven to 350°F. Spray an 8" × 8" baking pan with nonstick cooking spray.
2. Wash the eggplant and cut into slices about ¼ inch thick. Stir the dried basil, dried oregano, and garlic salt into the spaghetti sauce.
3. Lay out half the eggplant slices flat on the prepared baking pan. Spoon the spaghetti sauce over the top. Cover the eggplant with foil and bake for 20 minutes or until tender. Remove from the oven. Uncover and lay the mozzarella slices on top.
4. Bake another 3–5 minutes, until the cheese melts. Sprinkle with Parmesan cheese and serve.

Ⓥ Indian Tofu Palak

Serves 4

COST: $1.86
Per 1 cup serving
Calories: 195
Fat: 10g
Carbohydrates: 16g
Protein: 15g
Fiber: 8g
Sugar: 2g
Sodium: 597mg

3 cloves garlic, minced
1 block firm tofu, cut into small cubes
2 tablespoons olive oil
2 tablespoons nutritional yeast
½ teaspoon onion powder

4 bunches fresh spinach
3 tablespoons water
1 tablespoon curry powder
2 teaspoons cumin
½ teaspoon salt
½ cup plain soy yogurt

1. Heat garlic and tofu in olive oil over low heat and add nutritional yeast and onion powder, stirring to coat tofu. Heat for 2–3 minutes until tofu is lightly browned.
2. Add spinach, water, curry, cumin, and salt, stirring well to combine. Once spinach starts to wilt, add soy yogurt and heat just until spinach is fully wilted and soft.

Serves 8

COST: $0.75

Per 1 burger
Calories: 195
Fat: 3g
Carbohydrates: 32g
Protein: 7g
Fiber: 2g
Sugar: 3g
Sodium: 345mg

6 ounces firm tofu
6 tablespoons quick-cooking oats
2 tablespoons finely chopped onion
3 tablespoons Worcestershire sauce
⅛ teaspoon (or to taste) chili powder
1 egg
2 teaspoons olive oil
1 cup crushed tomatoes
2 tablespoons (or to taste) white vinegar
2 teaspoons (or to taste) granulated sugar
8 English muffins

1. Drain the tofu and crumble. Stir in the oats, onion, Worcestershire sauce, and chili powder. Add the egg and mix together with your hands to make sure the tofu is thoroughly mixed with the other ingredients.
2. Heat the olive oil in a frying pan. Form the tofu mixture into balls approximately the size of large golf balls and flatten with the palm of your hand. Add the burgers to the frying pan, using a spatula to gently flatten them and push together any portions that separate from the main burger. Cook the burgers for 3–4 minutes on each side, until browned.
3. Heat the crushed tomatoes, vinegar, and sugar in a small saucepan. Taste and adjust the seasoning if desired. Keep warm on low heat while toasting the English muffins.
4. Split the muffins in half and toast. Serve open-faced, with a portion of the tomato mixture spooned onto one muffin half and the burger on the other.

Types of Tofu

Made from cooked, coagulated soybeans and little else, tofu is a minimally processed, low-fat source of calcium and protein. Plain tofu comes in either firm, extrafirm, or silken (also called silk or soft tofu), and many grocers stock a variety of prebaked or flavored tofu. Firm or extra-firm tofu is used in stir-fries and baked dishes when you want the tofu to hold shape. For creamy sauces, use silken tofu.

Ⓥ The Easiest Black Bean Burger Recipe in the World

Yields 6 patties

COST: $0.75

Per 1 burger
Calories: 155
Fat: 8g
Carbohydrates: 21g
Protein: 7g
Fiber: 4g
Sugar: 1.5g
Sodium: 559mg

1 15-ounce can black beans, drained
3 tablespoons minced onions
1 teaspoon salt
1½ teaspoons garlic powder

2 teaspoons parsley
1 teaspoon chili powder
⅔ cup flour
¼ cup oil for pan-frying

1. Process the black beans in a blender or food processor until halfway mashed, or mash with a fork.
2. Add minced onions, salt, garlic powder, parsley, and chili powder, and mash to combine.
3. Add flour, a bit at a time, mashing together to combine. You may need a little bit more or less than ⅔ cup. Beans should stick together completely.
4. Form into patties and pan-fry in a bit of oil for 2–3 minutes on each side. Patties will appear to be done on the outside while still a bit mushy on the inside, so fry them a few minutes longer than you think they need.

Ⓥ Basic Baked Tempeh Patties

Serves 2

COST: $1.35

Per 1 patty
Calories: 278
Fat: 16g
Carbohydrates: 13g
Protein: 23g
Fiber: 0g
Sugar: 0g
Sodium: 959mg

1 8-ounce package tempeh
1 cup vegetable broth plus 2 tablespoons
3 tablespoons soy sauce

2 tablespoons apple cider vinegar
3 cloves garlic, minced
2 teaspoons sesame oil

1. Simmer tempeh in 1 cup water or vegetable broth for 10 minutes; drain well.
2. Whisk together remaining ingredients, including 2 tablespoons vegetable broth, and marinate tempeh for at least 1 hour or overnight.
3. Preheat oven to 375°F and transfer tempeh to a lightly greased baking sheet.
4. Bake for 10–12 minutes on each side.

Ⓥ Tofu BBQ Sauce "Steaks"

Serves 3

COST: $0.98

Per 10-oz. serving
Calories: 240
Fat: 13g
Carbohydrates: 19g
Protein: 11g
Fiber: 1g
Sugar: 13g
Sodium: 885mg

⅓ cup barbecue sauce
¼ cup water
2 teaspoons balsamic vinegar
2 tablespoons soy sauce
1–2 tablespoons hot sauce (or to taste)

2 teaspoons sugar
2 blocks extra-firm tofu, well pressed
½ onion, chopped
2 tablespoons olive oil

1. In a small bowl, whisk together the barbecue sauce, water, vinegar, soy sauce, hot sauce, and sugar until well combined. Set aside.
2. Slice pressed tofu into ¼-inch-thick strips.
3. Sauté onions in oil, and carefully add tofu. Fry tofu on both sides until lightly golden brown, about 2 minutes on each side.
4. Reduce heat and add barbecue sauce mixture, stirring to coat tofu well. Cook over medium-low heat until sauce absorbs and thickens, about 5–6 minutes.

Tofu Versus Seitan

This recipe, like many pan-fried or stir-fried tofu recipes, will also work well with seitan, though seitan needs a bit longer to cook all the way through; otherwise, it ends up tough and chewy. Seitan is not typically more expensive, however it can be more difficult to find.

Manchego-Potato Tacos with Pickled Jalapeños

Serves 8

COST: $1.52

Per 1 taco
Calories: 207
Fat: 11g
Carbohydrates: 18g
Protein: 7g
Fiber: 3g
Sugar: 1g
Sodium: 402mg

1 cup leftover mashed potatoes
8 soft corn tortillas
¼ pound Spanish Manchego cheese, cut into 16 small sticks

16 slices pickled jalapeño pepper (available in Mexican sections and ethnic specialty stores)
4 tablespoons unsalted butter

1. Spoon 1 tablespoon of mashed potato into the center of each tortilla. Flatten out the potatoes, leaving a 1-inch border. Lay 2 pieces of Manchego and 2 pieces pickled jalapeño onto each tortilla, then fold closed into a half-moon shape.
2. In a skillet over medium heat, melt half of the butter. Gently lay 4 tacos into the pan, and cook until nicely browned, about 3–4 minutes on each side. Drain on paper towels. Repeat with remaining tacos. Snip tacos in half before serving with salsa.

Ⓥ Ratatouille with Cannellini Beans

Serves 6

COST: $2.68

Per 1 cup
Calories: 167
Fat: 5g
Carbohydrates: 24g
Protein: 8g
Fiber: 8g
Sugar: 8g
Sodium: 405mg

2 tablespoons olive oil
1 large onion, diced
2 medium zucchini, diced
2 medium yellow squash, diced
1 small eggplant, diced
1 bell pepper, diced
2 cups cannellini beans, cooked
1 tablespoon flour

3 tomatoes, seeded, and cut into 6 pieces
2 teaspoons dried herbes de Provence (or a combination of oregano, thyme, rosemary, marjoram, savory, and/or lavender)
1 teaspoon salt
Freshly ground black pepper

1. Heat the olive oil in a heavy-bottomed Dutch oven until hot, but not smoky. Add onion; cook until translucent, about 5 minutes. Combine the zucchini, yellow squash, eggplant, and bell pepper in a large paper bag; dust with flour, fold bag closed, and shake to coat. Add floured vegetables to the pot, along with the tomatoes, herbs, salt, and pepper.
2. Reduce heat to a simmer, cover, and cook gently for 1 hour, until all vegetables are tender. Serve hot or at room temperature.

Eggplant Rolatine

Serves 8

1 large eggplant, sliced length-wise into even ⅛-inch slices (as thick as the cover of a hardcover book)
Flour for dredging
Egg wash of 6 beaten eggs, mixed with ½ cup water
2 cups bread crumbs
Oil for frying

1 pound ricotta cheese
8 ounces shredded mozzarella cheese
½ cup grated Parmesan
Salt and pepper
1½ pounds fresh spinach, washed and cooked
4 cups tomato sauce

1. Bread and fry the eggplant: Dip a slice of eggplant in the flour to coat both sides; shake off excess flour, submerge in egg wash, shake off excess, and coat in bread crumbs, pressing to make sure they adhere well. Place on a holding tray, and repeat with remaining slices. Heat oil to 350°F (a piece of vegetable should sizzle visibly when dropped into the oil). Fry the breaded eggplant slices for 1 minute per side, dripping any excess oil off before stacking them between layers of paper towels.

2. Fill and roll: Heat oven to 350°F. Combine the 3 cheeses in a mixing bowl, and season lightly with salt and pepper. Place 1 teaspoon cooked spinach and a generous teaspoon of cheese mixture at the wide end of a fried eggplant slice. Roll away from yourself, jellyroll style, and place into a baking dish, with the seam on the bottom. Repeat with remaining eggplant and fillings, lining the finished roulades close together in the baking dish.

3. Bake until cheeses are visibly hot, and the edges begin to brown lightly. Serve on a pool of tomato sauce, garnished with basil leaves. One piece per appetizer portion, 2 per main course.

Ⓥ Grilled Marinated Portobello Mushrooms

Serves 4

COST: $2.29

Per 1 mushroom
Calories: 100
Fat: 7g
Carbohydrates: 7g
Protein: 3g
Fiber: 2g
Sugar: 5g
Sodium: 462mg

4 large portobello (4–6 inches in diameter) mushrooms, stems removed
1 cup extra-virgin olive oil

1 cup red wine vinegar
2 tablespoons soy sauce
1 tablespoon sugar
½ cup chopped fresh chives

1. Brush any dirt from the mushrooms, but do not wash them under water. Whisk together the olive oil, vinegar, soy sauce, sugar, and chives. In a shallow dish, pour the marinade over the mushrooms; marinate 10 minutes, turning occasionally.
2. Grill 2–3 minutes on each side. Serve whole or sliced. Sauce with leftover marinade, or save the marinade for another batch.

Ⓥ Black Bean and Butternut Squash Chili

Serves 4

COST: $1.87

Per 1½ cups
Calories: 339
Fat: 8g
Carbohydrates: 55g
Protein: 16g
Fiber: 16g
Sugar: 12g
Sodium: 832mg

1 onion, chopped
3 cloves garlic, minced
2 tablespoons oil
1 medium butternut squash, chopped into chunks
2 15-ounce cans black beans, drained and rinsed
1 28-ounce can diced tomatoes, undrained

¾ cup vegetable broth
1 tablespoon chili powder
1 teaspoon cumin
¼ teaspoon cayenne pepper, or to taste
½ teaspoon salt
2 tablespoons chopped fresh cilantro

1. In a large stockpot, sauté onion and garlic in oil until soft, about 4 minutes. Reduce heat and add remaining ingredients, except cilantro.
2. Cover and simmer for 25 minutes. Uncover and simmer another 5 minutes. Top with fresh cilantro just before serving.

Ⓥ Beer-Battered Tofu Fillet

Serves 8

COST: $0.64

Per 6-oz. serving
Calories: 289
Fat: 16g
Carbohydrates: 21g
Protein: 12g
Fiber: 1g
Sugar: 1.4g
Sodium: 306mg

2 teaspoons garlic powder
2 teaspoons onion powder
2 teaspoons paprika
1 teaspoon salt
½ teaspoon black pepper

3 blocks extra-firm tofu,
  chopped into chunks
1 12-ounce bottle of beer
1⅓ cups flour
½ cup oil for frying

1. Combine the garlic powder, onion powder, paprika, salt, and pepper. Sprinkle the mixture over the tofu, gently pressing to stick.
2. Pour the beer into a large bowl and add flour, stirring to combine.
3. Dip the tofu in the beer batter, then fry in plenty of oil on both sides until crispy.

Ⓥ Polenta and Chili Casserole

Serves 4

COST: $0.64

Per 2 cups
Calories: 405
Fat: 7g
Carbohydrates: 59g
Protein: 16g
Fiber: 13g
Sugar: 7g
Sodium: 779mg

6 cups vegetarian chili (about
  3 cans if you're using
  store-bought)
2 cups diced veggie mixture,
  any kind

1 cup cornmeal
2½ cups water
2 tablespoons vegan margarine
1 tablespoon chili powder

1. Combine vegetarian chili and vegetables, and spread in the bottom of a lightly greased casserole dish.
2. Preheat oven to 375°F.
3. Over low heat, combine cornmeal and water in a saucepan. Simmer, stirring frequently, for 10 minutes. Stir in vegan margarine.
4. Spread cornmeal mixture over chili and sprinkle the top with chili powder. Bake uncovered for 20–25 minutes.

Spinach and Feta Pie

Serves 8

COST: $2.27

Per 1 slice
Calories: 397
Fat: 30g
Carbohydrates: 20g
Protein: 12g
Fiber: 2g
Sugar: 2g
Sodium: 545mg

1 bunch fresh spinach (about 4 cups)
3 tablespoons olive oil
1 yellow onion, chopped
1 cup grated Swiss cheese
2 eggs
1¼ cups light cream
¼ teaspoon salt
¼ teaspoon freshly ground black pepper
Pinch of nutmeg
¼ cup grated Parmesan cheese
1 10-inch deep-dish pie crust, prebaked 5 minutes at 375°F
6 ounces feta cheese, crumbled
2 medium tomatoes, sliced

1. Preheat oven to 350°F. Wash and stem the spinach; steam until wilted. Squeeze out excess water and chop. Heat the olive oil in a small skillet, and cook the onion until golden, about 7 minutes; toss with the spinach. Stir in the Swiss cheese.
2. Combine the eggs, cream, salt, pepper, nutmeg, and Parmesan cheese in a blender. Blend 1 minute. Spread the spinach mixture into the crust. Top with feta cheese and decorate with tomatoes if desired. Pour on the egg mixture, pressing through with your fingers to make sure it soaks through to the crust.
3. Bake 45 minutes, until a knife inserted in the pie comes out clean. Serve hot or room temperature.

Fried Eggplant Parmigiana

Serves 8

COST: $1.58

Per 8-oz. serving
Calories: 349
Fat: 18g
Carbohydrates: 28g
Protein: 18g
Fiber: 3g
Sugar: 6g
Sodium: 710mg

¼ cup oil for frying
1 medium eggplant (about 1 pound), sliced thin
½ cup flour
3 eggs, beaten, mixed with ½ cup water
2 cups bread crumbs
1 28-ounce jar store-bought marinara sauce
¾ pound part-skim mozzarella cheese, shredded
Whole fresh basil leaves

1. Heat the oil in a heavy skillet or fryer (about ½" deep) until a piece of vegetable sizzles when added. Dip a piece of eggplant in the flour and shake off excess; dip it in the egg mixture and shake off excess, then press it into the bread crumbs. Repeat with remaining slices of eggplant. Fry the slices until golden, about 3 minutes each; drain on a rack or on paper towels.
2. Preheat oven to 350°F. Line the slices into a baking dish. Top each with a teaspoon of tomato sauce and a small mound of shredded cheese. Bake until cheese is melted, browning, and bubbly, about 15 minutes. Serve with tomato sauce on the side, garnished with chopped parsley or leaves of fresh basil.

Cheese Soufflé

Serves 6

COST: $0.49

Per 4-oz. soufflé
Calories: 244
Fat: 17g
Carbohydrates: 9g
Protein: 12g
Fiber: 0g
Sugar: 3g
Sodium: 331mg

¼ cup unsalted butter
½ cup flour
½ teaspoon table salt
½ teaspoon paprika
Dash of cayenne or pepper
  sauce

2 cups milk
¼ pound sharp Cheddar
  cheese, diced
8 large eggs, separated

1. Preheat oven to 375°F. Butter a 10-inch soufflé dish, and coat the inside with flour. Melt ½ cup butter in a double boiler or a steel bowl, set over a pot of simmering water. Add the flour, salt, paprika, and cayenne (or pepper sauce); mix well. Gradually stir in the milk with a stiff whisk or wooden spoon. Cook, stirring constantly, until the mixture has become very thick. Stir in the cheese, and continue stirring until all cheese is melted. Remove from the heat.

2. Beat the yolks until they are lemon colored, then gradually stir them into the cheese sauce. In a very clean bowl, whip the egg whites until they are stiff, but not dry. Gently fold them into the cheese sauce, and then pour this batter into the soufflé dish. At this point, the soufflé may be covered and refrigerated for up to 1 hour, or baked right away.

3. Bake at 375°F for 10 minutes. Reduce heat to 300°F, and bake for 25 minutes more. Serve immediately. Add a grain, such as quinoa, and at least 1 cup of vegetables for a complete meal.

Chickpea, Parsnip, and Carrot Bake

Serves 4

COST: $1.33

Per 10-oz. serving
Calories: 275
Fat: 8g
Carbohydrates: 43g
Protein: 9g
Fiber: 12g
Sugar: 12g
Sodium: 487mg

1 pound carrots, peeled, cut roughly into 2½" × ½" batons
8 ounces parsnips, peeled, cut roughly into 2½" × ½" batons
2 cups chickpeas, cooked

¾ cup vegetable stock
2 tablespoons butter, chopped
½ teaspoon salt
Chopped fresh tarragon
Freshly ground black pepper

Preheat oven to 375°F. Place carrots, parsnips, chickpeas, stock, butter, and salt into a shallow baking dish. Cover with aluminum foil and bake until the vegetables are soft, about 45 minutes. Uncover and bake until vegetables brown lightly, 10–15 minutes more. Sprinkle with chervil and black pepper before serving.

Ⓥ Chickpea Soft Tacos

Serves 4

COST: $1.37

Per 1 taco
Calories: 264
Fat: 5g
Carbohydrates: 45g
Protein: 11g
Fiber: 9g
Sugar: 8g
Sodium: 461mg

2 cups (1½ cans) chickpeas, cooked
½ cup water
1 6-ounce can tomato paste
1 tablespoon chili powder

1 teaspoon garlic powder
½ teaspoon onion powder
½ teaspoon cumin
¼ cup chopped fresh cilantro
4 flour tortillas

1. Combine chickpeas, water, tomato paste, chili powder, garlic powder, onion powder, and cumin in a large skillet. Cover and simmer for 10 minutes, stirring occasionally. Uncover and simmer another 1–2 minutes or until most of the liquid is absorbed.
2. Uncover and use a fork or potato masher to mash the chickpeas until half mashed. Stir in fresh cilantro. Spoon mixture into flour tortillas, add toppings, and wrap.

Ⓥ Portobello and Pepper Fajitas

Serves 2

COST: $3.50

Per 1 fajita
Calories: 287
Fat: 16g
Carbohydrates: 30g
Protein: 7g
Fiber: 6g
Sugar: 9g
Sodium: 214mg

2 tablespoons olive oil
2 large portobello mushrooms, cut into strips
1 green bell pepper, cut into strips
1 red bell pepper, cut into strips

1 onion, cut into strips
¾ teaspoon chili powder
¼ teaspoon cumin
Dash hot sauce
1 tablespoon chopped fresh cilantro
2 flour tortillas, warmed

1. Heat olive oil in a large skillet and add mushrooms, bell peppers, and onion. Allow to cook for 3–5 minutes until vegetables are almost done.
2. Add chili powder, cumin, and hot sauce, and stir to combine. Cook for 2–3 minutes until mushrooms and peppers are soft. Remove from heat and stir in fresh cilantro.
3. Layer the mushrooms and peppers in flour tortillas.

Ⓥ Mexico City Protein Bowl

Serves 2

COST: $3.50

Per 1 bowl
Calories: 436
Fat: 11g
Carbohydrates: 64g
Protein: 21g
Fiber: 18g
Sugar: 9g
Sodium: 232mg

½ block firm tofu, diced small
1 scallion, chopped
1 tablespoon olive oil
½ cup peas
½ cup corn kernels

½ teaspoon chili powder
2 cups black beans, canned
2 corn tortillas
Hot sauce, to taste

1. Heat tofu and scallion in olive oil for 2–3 minutes, then add peas, corn, and chili powder. Cook another 1–2 minutes, stirring frequently.
2. Reduce heat to medium low, and add black beans. Heat for 4–5 minutes until well combined and heated through.
3. Place 2 corn tortillas in the bottom of a bowl, and spoon beans and tofu over the top. Season with hot sauce to taste.

Ⓥ Basic Homemade Seitan

Serves 8

COST: $0.24
Per 3-oz. serving
Calories: 28
Fat: 0g
Carbohydrates: 3g
Protein: 6g
Fiber: 0g
Sugar: 1g
Sodium: 119mg

1 cup vital wheat gluten
1 teaspoon onion powder
1 teaspoon garlic powder

2 tablespoons soy sauce
6¾ cups strong vegetable
 broth, divided

1. Combine the vital wheat gluten with the onion powder and garlic powder. In a separate bowl, combine the soy sauce and ¾ cup vegetable broth.
2. Slowly add the soy sauce and vegetable broth to the wheat gluten mixture, mixing with your hands until all of the flour is combined. You'll have one big rubbery ball of dough, and you may need a bit more or less than ¾ cup broth.
3. Knead the dough a few times to get an even texture. Let dough rest for a few minutes, then knead again for 1–2 minutes.
4. Divide dough into 3 (or more) pieces and stretch and press to about 1-inch thickness.
5. Slowly simmer in 6 cups vegetable broth for 45–60 minutes over low heat.

Seitan Tips

Shop for vital wheat gluten, also called wheat gluten flour, at your natural-foods store in the bulk section or baking aisle. Note that this recipe is for a basic, raw seitan. It won't be too tasty if you eat it plain, as it still needs to be cooked, even after all that boiling!

Ⓥ BBQ Seitan

Serves 6

COST: $0.51
Per ½ cup
Calories: 190
Fat: 5g
Carbohydrates: 18g
Protein: 15g
Fiber: 2g
Sugar: 12g
Sodium: 477mg

1 package prepared seitan, chopped into thin strips (about 2 cups)
1 large onion, chopped
3 cloves garlic, minced

2 tablespoons oil
1 cup barbecue sauce
2 tablespoons water

1. Heat seitan, onions, and garlic in oil, stirring frequently, until onions are just soft and seitan is lightly browned.
2. Reduce heat to medium low and stir in barbecue sauce and water. Allow to simmer, stirring to coat seitan, until most of the liquid has been absorbed, about 10 minutes.

Seitan Sandwiches

Pile BBQ Seitan on top of sourdough along with some vegan mayonnaise, lettuce, and tomato: This makes a perfect sandwich. You can also melt some vegan cheese for a simple Philly-style sandwich, or pile on the vegan Thousand Island and sauerkraut for a seitan Reuben.

🅥 Greek Seitan Gyros

Serves 6

COST: $1.48

Per 1 gyro
Calories: 291
Fat: 9g
Carbohydrates: 40g
Protein: 23g
Fiber: 4g
Sugar: 5g
Sodium: 374mg

1 16-ounce package seitan, thinly sliced
2 tablespoons oil
¾ teaspoon paprika
½ teaspoon dried parsley
¼ teaspoon garlic powder
¼ teaspoon oregano
Salt and pepper, to taste

6 pitas
2 tomatoes, sliced thin
1 onion, chopped
½ head iceberg lettuce, shredded
1 cup nondairy sour cream

1. Sauté seitan in oil and coat well with seasonings. Heat until seitan is lightly browned and spices are fragrant, about 5–7 minutes.
2. Top each pita with a portion of seitan, tomatoes, onion, lettuce, and about 2 tablespoons non-dairy sour cream; fold in half to eat.

🅥 Tandoori Seitan

Serves 6

COST: $1.26

Per 4-oz. serving
Calories: 148
Fat: 6g
Carbohydrates: 7g
Protein: 16g
Fiber: 2g
Sugar: 3g
Sodium: 238mg

⅔ cup soy yogurt
2 tablespoons lemon juice
1½ tablespoons tandoori spice blend
½ teaspoon cumin
½ teaspoon garlic powder
¼ teaspoon salt

1 16-ounce package prepared seitan, chopped
1 bell pepper, chopped
1 onion, chopped
1 tomato, chopped
2 tablespoons oil

1. Whisk together the yogurt, lemon juice, and all the spices in a shallow bowl or pan and add seitan. Allow to marinate for at least 1 hour. Reserve marinade.
2. Sauté pepper, onion, and tomato in oil over medium heat until just barely soft. Reduce heat to low and add seitan. Cook, tossing seitan occasionally, for 8–10 minutes. Serve topped with extra marinade.

Ⓥ Seitan Buffalo Wings

Serves 4

⅓ cup coconut oil
⅓ cup hot sauce
1 cup flour
1 teaspoon garlic powder
1 teaspoon onion powder

¼ teaspoon pepper
½ cup soy milk
4 tablespoons oil for frying
1 16-ounce package seitan, chopped

1. Over low heat, combine the coconut oil and hot sauce, just until oil is melted. Set aside.
2. In a small bowl, combine the flour, garlic powder, onion powder, and pepper; place soy milk in a separate bowl. Heat oil in a skillet or stockpot over medium heat.
3. Dip each piece of seitan in the soy milk, then dredge in flour mixture. Carefully place in hot oil and deep-fry in oil until lightly golden brown on all sides, about 4–5 minutes. Coat fried seitan with coconut oil and hot sauce mixture.

Baked, Not Fried

This is, admittedly, not the healthiest of vegan recipes, but you can cut some of the fat out by skipping the breading and deep-frying. Instead, lightly brown the seitan in a bit of oil, then coat with the sauce. Alternatively, bake the seitan with the sauce for 25 minutes at 325°F.

CHAPTER 8

Desserts

You come home from class and need a quick bite. You've just finished a vegetarian entrée and want to finish the meal off with a delicious dessert. You're halfway through an all-nighter and you're just really in the mood for brownies. Look no further than this chapter filled with delicious, easy-to-make desserts—all for less than $5 a serving! After all, pretty much everyone loves something sweet, and with recipes like Double Chocolate Chip Peppermint Drop Cookies, No-Bake Cocoa Balls, and Frozen Cappuccino Dessert, this chapter will definitely hit your sweet spot!

Basic Rice Krispies Squares

Yields about 24 squares

COST: $0.12
Per 1 square
Calories: 80
Fat: 2.5g
Carbohydrates: 14g
Protein: 1g
Fiber: 0g
Sugar: 6g
Sodium: 60mg

⅓ cup butter
4½ cups mini vegan
  marshmallows

6 cups Kellogg's Rice Krispies
  cereal

1. In a heavy skillet, melt the butter and marshmallows over low heat (otherwise the melted marshmallows will stick to the pan). When the marshmallows have completely melted, remove from heat.
2. Stir in the cereal and mix thoroughly. Spread out the mixture evenly in a 9" × 13" pan. Serve warm, or cool in the refrigerator for 1 hour first. Cut into squares before serving.

Simple Fruit Parfait

Serves 6

COST: $0.75
Per 1 parfait
Calories: 70
Fat: 1.5g
Carbohydrates: 13g
Protein: 5g
Fiber: 3g
Sugar: 5
Sodium: 35mg

1 cup sliced banana
1 cup fresh blueberries
1 cup vanilla-flavored Greek
  yogurt

1 tablespoon lime juice
¼ cup unsweetened coconut
  flakes

Divide the sliced banana among 6 wine or parfait glasses, then add the blueberries, and finally the yogurt. Drizzle with the lime juice and sprinkle the coconut flakes over the top. Chill in the refrigerator, and serve.

Ⓥ Pineapple Cherry "Dump" Cake

Serves 8

COST: $1.75

Per 1 slice
Calories: 498
Fat: 16g
Carbohydrates: 13g
Protein: 4g
Fiber: 1g
Sugar: 36g
Sodium: 594mg

1 20-ounce can crushed pineapple, undrained
1 20-ounce can cherry pie filling

1 box vegan vanilla cake mix
½ cup vegan margarine, melted

1. Preheat oven according to directions on cake mix box and lightly grease and flour a large cake pan.
2. Dump the pineapple into the cake pan, then dump the pie filling, and add the powdered cake mix on top.
3. Drizzle the cake mix with vegan margarine.
4. Bake according to instructions on cake mix package.

How to Grease and Flour a Cake Pan

Especially with lower-fat cake recipes such as this one, you'll want a well-greased and floured pan to prevent the cake from sticking. A nonstick spray works just as well as a tablespoon or so of melted margarine or cooking oil. Coat the pan well, including the sides. Then, coat with a light dusting of flour, shaking the pan to cover all the edges.

Peanut Butter Rice Krispies

Yields about 20 squares (20 servings)

COST: $0.41
Per 1 square
Calories: 240
Fat: 11g
Carbohydrates: 36g
Protein: 4g
Fiber: 2g
Sugar: 28g
Sodium: 65mg

1 cup natural peanut butter
½ cup raw sugar
½ cup brown sugar
¾ cup honey

4 cups Kellogg's Rice Krispies cereal
1 tablespoon unsalted butter
1½ cups semisweet chocolate chips

1. Melt the peanut butter, sugars, and honey in a skillet over low heat, stirring continually. When the mixture is melted, gradually stir in the cereal.
2. Spread out the mixture evenly in a 9" × 9" baking pan.
3. Place the butter and chocolate chips in a metal bowl and place it on top of a saucepan filled halfway with nearly boiling water. Melt the butter and chocolate on low heat, stirring constantly to make sure the chocolate doesn't boil.
4. Spread the melted chocolate over the Rice Krispies mixture. Let cool and cut into squares.

Ⓥ Lemon Cranberry Sorbet

Serves 1

COST: $0.99
Per 1 sorbet
Calories: 250
Fat: 0g
Carbohydrates: 65g
Protein: 1g
Fiber: 5g
Sugar: 55g
Sodium: 0mg

1 cup (about 48) cranberries, washed and drained
½ teaspoon grated fresh lemon zest

¾ cup water, divided
4 tablespoons granulated sugar
2 tablespoons lemon juice

1. Place the cranberries, lemon zest , and ½ cup water in a small saucepan. Cook on medium heat until the cranberries pop, about 5–6 minutes. Gently mash the cranberries.
2. Stir in the sugar, lemon juice, and remaining water. Bring to a boil, stirring.
3. Remove from the heat and let cool. Pour into a serving bowl and place in the freezer until the sorbet is just starting to freeze, about 30 minutes.
4. Place in a blender or food processor and process until smooth. Freeze again.

Almond Fruit Cocktail Float

Serves 6

COST: $1.93

Per 1 square
Calories: 170
Fat: 0g
Carbohydrates: 33g
Protein: 9g
Fiber: 1g
Sugar: 10g
Sodium: 105mg

2 tablespoons unflavored vegetarian gelatin, such as agar flakes
1½ cups water
½ cup boiling water

2 cups evaporated milk
½ cup granulated sugar
1 tablespoon almond extract
1 15-ounce can fruit cocktail

1. In a medium-sized bowl, add the gelatin to ½ cup water and let it sit for 2–3 minutes to soften. Pour the ½ cup boiling water over the soaked gelatin and stir until dissolved.
2. Stir in the remaining 1 cup water, and the milk, sugar, and almond extract. Pour into a 9" × 9" pan. Chill in the refrigerator until firm.
3. To serve, cut the chilled gelatin into 1-inch squares and serve in individual serving bowls with the fruit cocktail over the top.

Old-Fashioned Baked Apples

Serves 4

COST: $1.13

Per 1 apple
Calories: 210
Fat: 11g
Carbohydrates: 38g
Protein: 1g
Fiber: 3g
Sugar: 34g
Sodium: 7mg

4 baking apples (Romes or Cortlands are good)
8 whole cloves
2 ounces butter (½ stick)

⅓ cup light brown sugar
½ teaspoon ground cinnamon or powdered sugar

1. Preheat oven to 350°F. Wash and dry apples thoroughly. Using a small knife, cut a divot from the top of the apples, leaving the stem intact. This "cover" will be replaced when baking. Scoop out the seeds and core with a melon baller or small spoon. Drop 2 cloves into each apple.
2. Knead together the butter and brown sugar, along with the cinnamon, until it is a paste. Divide equally over the scooped apples, leaving enough space to replace the tops.
3. Place apples in a baking dish with ½ cup water on the bottom. Bake for 1 hour. Sprinkle with cinnamon or powdered sugar before serving.

Ⓥ Chocolate Mocha Ice Cream

Serves 6

COST: $1.83
Per ¾ cup
Calories: 150
Fat: 8g
Carbohydrates: 15g
Protein: 5g
Fiber: 0g
Sugar: 10g
Sodium: 120mg

1 cup vegan chocolate chips
1 cup soy milk
1 12-ounce block silken tofu
⅓ cup sugar

2 tablespoons instant coffee
2 teaspoons vanilla
¼ teaspoon salt

1. Using a double boiler, or over very low heat, melt chocolate chips until smooth and creamy. Allow to cool slightly.
2. Blend together the soy milk, tofu, sugar, instant coffee, vanilla, and salt until very smooth and creamy, at least 2 minutes. Add melted chocolate chips, and process until smooth.
3. Transfer mixture to a large freezer-proof baking or casserole dish and freeze.
4. Stir every 30 minutes until a smooth ice cream forms, about 4 hours. If mixture gets too firm, transfer to a blender and process until smooth, then return to freezer.

Ⓥ Strawberry Coconut Ice Cream

Serves 6

COST: $1.55
Per ¾ cup
Calories: 475
Fat: 16g
Carbohydrates: 82g
Protein: 1g
Fiber: 2g
Sugar: 79g
Sodium: 120mg

2 cups coconut cream
1¾ cups frozen strawberries
¾ cup sugar

2 teaspoons vanilla
¼ teaspoon salt

1. Purée together all ingredients until smooth and creamy.
2. Transfer mixture to a large freezer-proof baking or casserole dish and freeze.
3. Stir every 30 minutes until a smooth ice cream forms, about 4 hours. If mixture gets too firm, transfer to a blender and process until smooth, then return to freezer.

No-Bake Cocoa Balls

Serves 6

COST: $2.15

Per 4 balls
Calories: 287
Fat: 16g
Carbohydrates: 29g
Protein: 7g
Fiber: 6.5g
Sugar: 20g
Sodium: 17mg

1 cup chopped pitted dates
1 cup cashews
¼ cup cocoa powder

1 tablespoon peanut butter
¼ cup coconut flakes

1. Cover dates in water and soak for about 10 minutes until softened. Drain.
2. Process dates, cashews, cocoa powder, and peanut butter in a food processor until combined and sticky. Add coconut flakes and process until coarse.
3. Shape into balls and chill. If mixture is too wet, add more nuts and coconut, or add just a touch of water if the mixture is dry and crumbly.

Baked Pears

Serves 4

COST: $1.21

Per 1 cup
Calories: 275
Fat: 6g
Carbohydrates: 58g
Protein: 3g
Fiber: 5g
Sugar: 47g
Sodium: 8mg

4 firm ripe pears
¼ cup brown sugar
4 tablespoons (or more to taste) red wine vinegar

4 tablespoons honey
¼ cup chopped walnuts
¼ cup unsweetened coconut flakes

1. Preheat oven to 350°F.
2. Cut the pears in half, remove the cores and stems, and cut into chunks. Sprinkle the brown sugar over a nonstick baking pan. Lay the pear slices on top of the brown sugar.
3. Mix together the red wine vinegar and honey. Drizzle the mixture over the pear slices. Sprinkle half the pear slices with the chopped walnuts and the other half with the coconut flakes.
4. Bake the pears for 25 minutes or until tender. Let cool briefly, and serve while still warm.

Ⓥ Summer Fruit Compote

Yields 2 cups

COST: $2.85

Per ½ cup
Calories: 325
Fat: 1g
Carbohydrates: 85g
Protein: 3g
Fiber: 8g
Sugar: 24g
Sodium: 21g

2 medium bananas
⅓ cup granulated sugar
1 cup water
1 teaspoon peeled and grated
  fresh ginger

¼ cup lemon juice
4 5-inch cinnamon sticks
3 cups dried tropical fruit

1. Peel and slice the bananas.
2. Cook the sugar and water in a saucepan over low heat, stirring to dissolve the sugar. Add the ginger, lemon juice, and cinnamon sticks. Increase heat to medium and bring to a boil. Reduce heat to low and simmer for 5 minutes.
3. Add the dried fruit and bananas. Return to a boil. Reduce heat to low, cover, and cook at a low simmer until the dried fruit is tender. Remove the cinnamon sticks.
4. Let cool briefly and serve warm, or refrigerate overnight and serve cold.

Mascarpone Pudding

Serves 6

COST: $1.24

Per ⅙ recipe
Calories: 340
Fat: 23g
Carbohydrates: 28g
Protein: 6g
Fiber: 2g
Sugar: 10g
Sodium: 50mg

1½ cups milk
1 cup long-grain rice
½ teaspoon ground cinnamon
1 teaspoon vanilla extract
¾ cup heavy cream

3 tablespoons granulated
  sugar
1 cup mascarpone
16 whole, unblanched almonds

1. In a medium-sized saucepan, add the milk to the rice. Stir in the cinnamon. Bring to a boil, uncovered, over medium heat. Cover, reduce heat to low, and simmer until cooked through, about 20 minutes, stirring occasionally.
2. Stir the vanilla extract into the heavy cream. Add to the rice, stirring. Continue cooking on low heat until the rice is tender. Remove from the heat.
3. Stir in the sugar and mascarpone. Spoon into dessert dishes and chill. Garnish with almonds.

Sour Cream Butter Cake

Serves 12

COST: $0.84

Per 1 slice
Calories: 292
Fat: 15g
Carbohydrates: 35g
Protein: 3g
Fiber: 1g
Sugar: 17g
Sodium: 156mg

4 egg yolks
⅔ cup sour cream
1½ teaspoons vanilla
2 cups sifted cake flour
1 cup sugar
½ teaspoon baking powder

½ teaspoon baking soda
½ teaspoon salt
6 ounces (1½ sticks) unsalted butter, softened to room temperature

1. Preheat oven to 350°F. Grease a 9-inch cake pan, dust it with flour, and line the bottom with waxed paper. In a bowl, whisk together the yolks, ¼ of the sour cream, and the vanilla. In a large, separate bowl, mix the flour, sugar, baking powder, baking soda, and salt; whisk vigorously to combine.
2. Add the butter and remaining sour cream to the flour mixture, and mix well until flour is completely moistened. Add the egg mixture to the flour mixture in 3 separate additions, mixing between each addition. Pour into prepared cake pan.
3. Bake in the middle of the oven until a toothpick inserted in the center comes out clean, usually about 35–40 minutes. Start checking at 25 minutes, since oven temperatures and ingredient characteristics vary, and it might be done quicker. Cool 10 minutes, then take out of pan and cool completely on a wire rack.

Serving Tips

If frosting cake, prepare by cutting cooled cakes laterally in half and frost both sections, then stack smooth sides, and refrigerate to set.

Easy Brown Betty

Serves 4

COST: $0.48

Per ¾ cup
Calories: 280
Fat: 13g
Carbohydrates: 39g
Protein: 2g
Fiber: 3g
Sugar: 29g
Sodium: 180mg

1 cup applesauce
2 tablespoons granulated sugar
4 tablespoons brown sugar
2 teaspoons lemon juice

⅛ teaspoon ground cinnamon, divided
⅛ teaspoon ground ginger
⅓ cup butter
2 cups graham cracker crumbs

1. Preheat oven to 350°F. Grease an 8" × 8" baking pan.
2. Combine the applesauce, granulated sugar, brown sugar, lemon juice, ⅛ teaspoon cinnamon, and the ground ginger. Set aside. Melt the butter. Toss the graham cracker crumbs with the melted butter. Press the graham cracker crumbs on the bottom of the prepared pan. Spread the applesauce mixture along the top. Sprinkle with the remaining cinnamon.
3. Cover with aluminum foil and bake for 30 minutes. Uncover and bake for another 5 minutes, to lightly brown the applesauce. Let cool on a rack. Cut into squares. Serve warm as is or topped with ice cream or whipped cream.

Ⓥ Foolproof Vegan Fudge

Yields 24 1-inch pieces

COST: $0.88

Per 1 inch piece of fudge
Calories: 210
Fat: 12g
Carbohydrates: 16g
Protein: 2g
Fiber: 1g
Sugar: 14g
Sodium: 89mg

⅓ cup vegan margarine
⅓ cup cocoa
⅓ cup soy cream
½ teaspoon vanilla

2 tablespoons peanut butter
3–3½ cups powdered sugar
¾ cup nuts, finely chopped

1. Lightly grease a small baking dish or square cake pan.
2. Using a double boiler, or over very low heat, melt the vegan margarine with the cocoa, soy cream, vanilla, and peanut butter.
3. Slowly incorporate powdered sugar until mixture is smooth, creamy, and thick. Stir in nuts.
4. Immediately transfer to pan and chill until completely firm, at least 2 hours.

Frozen Cappuccino Dessert

Serves 1

COST: $1.96

Per recipe
Calories: 160
Fat: 11g
Carbohydrates: 15g
Protein: 3g
Fiber: 0g
Sugar: 13g
Sodium: 90mg

1 cup cold brewed coffee
2 tablespoons plain cream
  cheese

1 tablespoon granulated sugar
2 teaspoons unsweetened
  cocoa powder

Combine all the ingredients in a blender and blend until smooth. Freeze for 2 hours, stirring occasionally. Serve chilled.

Strawberry Parfait

Serves 4

COST: $1.61

Per 1 parfait
Calories: 190
Fat: 4.5g
Carbohydrates: 36g
Protein: 0g
Fiber: 2g
Sugar: 23g
Sodium: 42mg

1 cup strawberries, rinsed,
  dried, and hulled
1½ cups Greek yogurt
½ cup strawberry preserves

4 whole strawberries, for
  garnish
Fresh mint leaves, for garnish

1. Slice the strawberries lengthwise and divide equally between 4 chilled martini glasses or ramekins.
2. Combine the yogurt with the strawberry preserves in a medium-sized mixing bowl and stir until evenly blended. Dollop the mixture on top of the fruit or use a piping bag to top each with a rosette. Garnish each with a whole strawberry and a fresh mint sprig.

Perfect Peanut Butter Cookies

Yields about 40 cookies

COST: $0.19
Per 1 cookie
Calories: 120
Fat: 8g
Carbohydrates: 10g
Protein: 2g
Fiber: 1g
Sugar: 6g
Sodium: 80mg

1 cup chunky natural peanut butter
¾ cup butter, room temperature
⅔ cup packed brown sugar
⅓ cup granulated sugar
½ cup chopped pecans
1 large egg
½ teaspoon vanilla extract
½ teaspoon baking soda
½ teaspoon salt
1½ cups all-purpose flour

1. Preheat oven to 350°F. Grease a 9" × 13" baking sheet.
2. In a large bowl, cream the peanut butter, butter, and the sugars. Stir in the pecans. Add the egg and vanilla extract.
3. In another bowl, sift the baking soda and salt into the flour. Gradually add it to the peanut butter mixture, stirring to mix. Roll the dough into balls about 1–1½ inches in diameter. Place on the prepared baking sheet, approximately 2 inches apart, and press down in the middle with a fork.
4. Bake for 12 minutes or until a toothpick inserted into the middle comes out clean. Let cool and store in a sealed container.

Ⓥ Classic Chocolate Chip Cookies

Yields about 24 cookies

COST: $0.31
Per 1 cookie
Calories: 161
Fat: 7g
Carbohydrates: 10g
Protein: 2g
Fiber: 1g
Sugar: 19g
Sodium: 232mg

⅔ cup vegan margarine
⅔ cup sugar
⅔ cup brown sugar
⅓ cup applesauce
1½ teaspoons vanilla
Egg replacer for 2 eggs
2½ cups flour
1 teaspoon baking soda
½ teaspoon baking powder
1 teaspoon salt
⅔ cup quick-cooking oats
1½ cups chocolate chips

1. Preheat oven to 375°F.
2. In a large mixing bowl, cream together the vegan margarine and white sugar, then mix in brown sugar, applesauce, vanilla, and egg replacer.
3. In a separate bowl, combine the flour, baking soda, baking powder, and salt, then combine with the wet ingredients. Mix well.
4. Stir in oats and chocolate chips just until combined.
5. Drop by generous spoonfuls onto a baking sheet, and bake for 10–12 minutes.

Double Chocolate Chip Peppermint Drop Cookies

Yields about 4 dozen cookies

COST: $0.12

Per 1 cookie
Calories: 60
Fat: 3.5g
Carbohydrates: 10g
Protein: 1g
Fiber: 1g
Sugar: 6g
Sodium: 40mg

½ cup, plus 2 tablespoons butter, room temperature
⅔ cup brown sugar
⅓ cup granulated sugar
2 tablespoons cocoa powder
1 egg
1 teaspoon vanilla extract

1 teaspoon peppermint extract
½ teaspoon baking soda
½ teaspoon salt
1½ cups all-purpose flour
1 cup semisweet chocolate chips

1. Preheat oven to 350°F.
2. In a large bowl, cream the butter with the sugars and cocoa powder.
3. Add the egg, vanilla extract, and peppermint extract.
4. In another bowl, sift the baking soda and salt into the flour. Gradually mix it into the butter and sugar. Stir in the chocolate chips.
5. Drop the cookies by teaspoonful onto an ungreased baking sheet, placed well apart (about 15 cookies per baking sheet). Bake for 10–12 minutes, depending on how crispy you like them.

Test Your Cookie IQ

Drops, bars, icebox cookies—it can all get a little confusing. Drop cookies have a wetter batter than traditional cookies. They are "dropped" from a teaspoon onto a baking sheet. Icebox or refrigerator cookies consist of cookie dough that can be refrigerated before cooking—a great idea if you want to prepare cookie dough ahead of time for quick baking later. To make bar cookies, simply spread cookie dough batter into a shallow pan, and then cut into bars after the dough is baked.

Easy Banana Date Cookies

Serves 12

COST: $0.54

Per 1 cookie
Calories: 77
Fat: 3g
Carbohydrates: 14g
Protein: 1g
Fiber: 2g
Sugar: 10g
Sodium: 2mg

1 cup chopped pitted dates
1 banana (medium ripe)

¼ teaspoon vanilla
1¾ cups coconut flakes

1. Preheat oven to 375°F. Cover dates in water and soak for about 10 minutes until softened. Drain.
2. Process together the dates, banana, and vanilla in a food processor until almost smooth. Stir in coconut flakes by hand until thick. You may need a little more or less than 1¾ cups.
3. Drop by generous tablespoonfuls onto a cookie sheet. Bake 10–12 minutes, or until done. Cookies will be soft and chewy.

Oatmeal Cranberry Chews

Yields about 4 dozen cookies

COST: $0.09

Per 1 cookie
Calories: 70
Fat: 4g
Carbohydrates: 9g
Protein: 1g
Fiber: 0.5g
Sugar: 5g
Sodium: 20mg

1 cup butter
½ cup granulated sugar
½ cup brown sugar
1 or 2 eggs, as needed
½ teaspoon baking soda
½ teaspoon baking powder

¾ teaspoon ground cinnamon
½ teaspoon ground nutmeg
1 cup all-purpose flour
1½ cups quick-cooking
  oatmeal
½ cup dried cranberries

1. Preheat oven to 350°F. Grease a 9" × 13" baking sheet.
2. In a large bowl, cream together the butter and sugars. Beat in 1 egg. In another bowl, sift the baking soda, baking powder, cinnamon, and nutmeg into the flour.
3. Add the flour to the butter mixture, blending thoroughly. Stir in the oatmeal and dried cranberries. If the cookie dough is too dry, beat in the remaining egg.
4. Drop a heaping teaspoon of dough onto the prepared baking sheet. Continue with the rest of the dough, placing the cookies about 2 inches apart. Bake for 10–12 minutes or until done.

Sweetheart Raspberry Lemon Cupcakes

Yields 18 cupcakes

COST: $0.25

Per 1 cupcake
Calories: 139
Fat: 5g
Carbohydrates: 21g
Protein: 2g
Fiber: 1g
Sugar: 8g
Sodium: 182mg

½ cup vegan margarine,
  softened
1 cup sugar
½ teaspoon vanilla
⅔ cup soy milk
3 tablespoons lemon juice
Zest from 2 lemons

1¾ cups flour
1½ teaspoons baking powder
½ teaspoon baking soda
¼ teaspoon salt
¾ cup diced raspberries,
  frozen

1. Preheat oven to 350°F and grease or line a cupcake tin.
2. Beat together the margarine and sugar until light and fluffy, then add vanilla, soy milk, lemon juice, and zest.
3. In a separate bowl, sift together the flour, baking powder, baking soda, and salt.
4. Combine flour mixture with wet ingredients just until mixed. Do not overmix. Gently fold in diced raspberries.
5. Fill cupcakes about ⅔ full with batter and bake immediately for 16–18 minutes or until done.

Raspberry Cream Cheese Frosting

To make Raspberry Cream Cheese Frosting simply combine half a container of vegan cream cheese with ½ cup raspberry jam and 6 tablespoons of softened vegan margarine. Beat until smooth, then add powdered sugar (you'll need about 2½ cups) until a creamy frosting forms.

Quick and Easy Brownies

Yields about 20 brownies

COST: $0.32

Per 1 brownie
Calories: 130
Fat: 9g
Carbohydrates: 14g
Protein: 2g
Fiber: 1g
Sugar: 10g
Sodium: 50mg

3 tablespoons unsweetened cocoa powder
1 cup granulated sugar
1 stick unsalted butter
¾ teaspoon vanilla extract
¼ cup egg substitute
½ teaspoon baking powder
¼ teaspoon salt
½ cup all-purpose flour
1 cup chopped walnuts

1. Preheat oven to 350°F. Grease a 9" × 9" pan.
2. In a large bowl, cream the cocoa and sugar into the butter until well blended. In a small bowl, stir the vanilla extract into the egg substitute. Beat the egg substitute into the cocoa mixture.
3. In another bowl, stir the baking powder and salt into the flour until well blended. Stir into the cocoa mixture, blending thoroughly. Stir in the chopped walnuts. Spread the brownie batter evenly in the prepared pan. Bake for 20–25 minutes, until done. Let cool and cut into bars.

Unsalted Butter Benefits

The name says it all—unsalted butter has no added salt. Cooks prefer it for baking, as salt can overpower butter's natural sweet flavor. The only drawback is that unsalted butter is more perishable—the salt in regular butter acts as a preservative. For long-term storage, keep it in your freezer.

Ⓥ Ginger Spice Cookies

Yields 1½ dozen cookies

COST: $0.15

Per 1 cookie
Calories: 130
Fat: 4g
Carbohydrates: 22g
Protein: 2g
Fiber: 1g
Sugar: 8g
Sodium: 178mg

⅓ cup vegan margarine,
  softened
½ cup maple syrup
⅓ cup molasses
¼ cup soy milk
2¼ cups flour

1 teaspoon baking powder
½ teaspoon baking soda
½ teaspoon cinnamon
½ teaspoon ginger
¼ teaspoon allspice
½ teaspoon salt

1. In a large mixing bowl, cream together the vegan margarine, maple syrup, molasses, and soy milk. In a separate bowl, sift together the flour, baking powder, baking soda, cinnamon, ginger, allspice, and salt.
2. Mix the flour and spices in with the wet ingredients until combined. Chill for 30 minutes.
3. Preheat oven to 375°F.
4. Roll dough into 1½-inch balls and place on cookie sheet. Flatten slightly, then bake 10–12 minutes, or until done.

Blender Chocolate Mousse for One

Serves 1

COST: $1.04

Per 1 recipe
Calories: 500
Fat: 46g
Carbohydrates: 24g
Protein: 5g
Fiber: 3.5g
Sugar: 15g
Sodium: 50mg

½ cup heavy whipping cream
2 tablespoons powdered sugar

2 tablespoons unsweetened
  cocoa powder
½ teaspoon vanilla extract

Combine all the ingredients, and blend with an electric blender until the mixture thickens. Chill before serving.

Lemon Crisp Cookies

Yields about 4 dozen cookies

1 cup granulated sugar
2 sticks unsalted butter,
  softened
3 teaspoons lemon juice
1 teaspoon lemon zest
1 large egg

¾ teaspoon baking soda
¼ teaspoon salt
2 cups all-purpose flour
⅓ cup (or more to taste) powdered sugar

1. Preheat oven to 350°F. Grease a 9" × 13" baking sheet.
2. In a large bowl, cream the granulated sugar into the butter until thoroughly blended. Blend in the lemon juice and zest. Beat in the egg.
3. In a separate bowl, add the baking soda and salt to the flour and stir until well blended.
4. Using an electric mixer set at low speed, gradually add the flour to the butter and sugar mixture until it is just blended into a soft dough. Drop a heaping teaspoon of dough onto the baking sheet. Continue with the remaining dough, placing the cookies about 1½ inches apart (about 15 cookies to a baking sheet).
5. Bake on the middle rack of the oven for 9–10 minutes or until a toothpick inserted into the center comes out clean. Be careful not to overcook. Dust the cookies with powdered sugar while still warm. Let cool for 2 minutes and then remove from the baking sheet.

Easy Apple Crisp

Yields 12 crisps

COST: $0.87

Per 4-oz. serving
Calories: 280
Fat: 8g
Carbohydrates: 52g
Protein: 2g
Fiber: 3g
Sugar: 28g
Sodium: 50mg

¾ cup all-purpose flour
¾ cup quick-cooking oats
¾ cup brown sugar
¼ cup granulated sugar
¾ teaspoon ground cinnamon

½ teaspoon ground nutmeg
½ teaspoon ground allspice
½ cup butter, softened
2 20-ounce cans apple pie
   filling

1. Preheat oven to 375°F. Grease a 9" × 9" baking pan.
2. Combine the flour, oats, brown sugar, granulated sugar, cinnamon, nutmeg, and allspice. Cut the softened butter into the dry ingredients with a knife. The mixture should be crumblike and slightly moist.
3. Spread 1 can of the apple pie filling on the prepared baking pan. Sprinkle a portion of the crumb mixture over the top until the pie filling is completely covered. Spread the second can of apple pie filling on top. Top with as much of the remaining crumb mixture as necessary to cover (a bit of crumb mixture may be left over).
4. Bake for 30 minutes or until browned. Let stand on a wire rack to cool for at least 15 minutes. Spoon into bowls and serve warm with ice cream.

Chocolate Biscotti

Yields about 40 cookies

COST: $0.20

Per 1 cookie
Calories: 100
Fat: 3.5g
Carbohydrates: 15g
Protein: 2g
Fiber: 0g
Sugar: 5g
Sodium: 35mg

5 eggs
1 teaspoon vanilla extract
2 cups all-purpose flour
1 teaspoon baking powder
⅛ teaspoon salt
1 cup granulated sugar

½ cup plus 1¾ tablespoons
   unsweetened cocoa powder
¾ cup semisweet chocolate
   chips
6 ounces white chocolate
1½ teaspoons shortening

1. Preheat oven to 325°F. Grease a large baking sheet.
2. In a small bowl, lightly beat the eggs with the vanilla extract. In a large bowl, combine the flour, baking powder, salt, sugar, and cocoa powder. Blend thoroughly. Add the beaten egg and blend to form a sticky dough. Stir in the chocolate chips.
3. Cut the dough in half. Flour your hands and shape each half into a 14-inch log. Place the logs on the prepared baking sheet and bake for 30 minutes or until a toothpick inserted in the center comes out clean. Let cool for 10 minutes.
4. Cut the dough diagonally into slices about ½ inch thick. Place cut-side down on 2 ungreased baking sheets. Bake for a total of 15 minutes, removing the baking sheets from the oven at the halfway point and turning the cookies over. Return to the oven, moving the cookie sheet that was on the top rack to the bottom rack and vice versa (this ensures the cookies cook evenly). Let cool.
5. Break the white chocolate into pieces. Melt the shortening and chocolate in a metal bowl placed on top of a heavy pot filled halfway with barely simmering water (or use the top of a double boiler if you have one). Melt over low heat, stirring regularly and making sure the chocolate doesn't burn. Use the back of a metal spatula or wooden spoon to spread the melted chocolate over one side of each biscotti. Let dry. Store the biscotti in a cookie tin or other airtight container.

Nanaimo Bars

Yields 20 bars

COST: $0.32

Per 1 bar
Calories: 230
Fat: 15g
Carbohydrates: 24g
Protein: 1g
Fiber: 1g
Sugar: 17g
Sodium: 45mg

2 ounces liquid egg substitute (equivalent of 1 egg)
½ teaspoon vanilla extract
2 sticks (1 cup) unsalted butter
3 teaspoons unsweetened cocoa powder
¼ cup granulated sugar
½ cup finely chopped pecans
½ cup sweetened coconut flakes

1 cup graham cracker crumbs
2 tablespoons custard powder
2 tablespoons butter
2 tablespoons, plus 1 teaspoon half-and-half
2 cups powdered sugar
4 squares (4 ounces) semi-sweet chocolate

1. Grease an 8" × 8" pan. In a small bowl, stir together the egg substitute and vanilla extract. Set aside.
2. For the bottom layer, melt 1 stick (½ cup) of the butter in a metal bowl placed over a saucepan filled halfway with barely simmering water. (You can also melt the butter in the top half of a double boiler.) Stir in the cocoa powder and granulated sugar. Remove from the heat. Stir in the egg substitute and vanilla extract mixture.
3. Stir in the chopped pecans, coconut, and graham cracker crumbs, mixing thoroughly. Press the mixture into the prepared pan, spreading it out evenly. Refrigerate until the next layer is completed.
4. For the middle layer, use a wooden spoon to cream the custard powder into 2 tablespoons of butter in a large bowl. Gradually add the half-and-half while creaming in the powdered sugar. Spread the icing evenly over the lower layer. Freeze for at least 2 hours.
5. To make the top layer, melt the remaining 1 stick butter and the chocolate in a metal bowl placed over a saucepan filled halfway with barely simmering water. Remove from the heat and allow to cool briefly. When the chocolate is just beginning to solidify, use a plastic spatula to spread it evenly over the middle layer. Return to the freezer and freeze for at least 2 hours. Cut into bars and serve.

Speedy Mocha "Mousse" Pudding

Serves 4

COST: $1.07

Per ¼ recipe
Calories: 410
Fat: 31g
Carbohydrates: 34g
Protein: 3g
Fiber: 2g
Sugar: 10g
Sodium: 270mg

2 cups heavy whipping cream
½ cup brewed instant coffee
½ cup powdered sugar
½ cup unsweetened cocoa
    powder
1 teaspoon vanilla extract

1 package instant vanilla
    pudding
½ cup (or to taste) prepared
    whipped cream
4 maraschino cherries

Combine the first six ingredients in a blender. Blend on low speed (prepare in two batches if necessary). Dish into parfait glasses and let sit for 5 minutes to allow the pudding to set. Just before serving, add the whipped cream and a maraschino cherry to the top of each.

Spoonful of Sugar?

Too much sugar may overwork your organs leaving you feeling tired and hungry, so make sure to only incorporate it into your balanced diet in small amounts. The American Heart Association recommends 9 teaspoons, or 32 grams, of sugar each day. The bottom line is to keep a treat a treat, so enjoy the recipes in this chapter after consuming an adequate amount of protein and fiber.

Chocolate Fudge Mousse with Coffee Whipped Cream

Serves 4

COST: $0.67
Per ¼ recipe
Calories: 310
Fat: 17g
Carbohydrates: 36g
Protein: 6g
Fiber: 2g
Sugar: 5g
Sodium: 180mg

1 package Jello sugar-free and fat-free instant chocolate fudge pudding mix
2 cups cold skim milk
¾ cup heavy cream, chilled
2–3 tablespoons granulated sugar
1 tablespoon prepared, very strong coffee, chilled

1. Combine the pudding mix and milk in a medium-sized mixing bowl. Use an electric mixer to beat for about 1½ minutes, until smooth. Equally divide the mixture between 4 parfait cups. Set aside for 5–7 minutes.
2. Put the cream in a medium-sized mixing bowl. Beat the cream until it just holds its shape. Sift the sugar over the cream and continue to beat until soft peaks form. Stir in the coffee and mix just until blended. Refrigerate until ready to serve.
3. To serve, top the pudding with equal amounts of coffee whipped cream. Served chilled.

Banana Mousse

Serves 6

COST: $0.52
Per ¾ cup mousse
Calories: 260
Fat: 22g
Carbohydrates: 16g
Protein: 2g
Fiber: 1g
Sugar: 9g
Sodium: 25mg

3 large bananas, mashed
2 cups whipping cream
3 tablespoons powdered sugar
2 tablespoons lemon juice
¼ teaspoon (or to taste) ground nutmeg
1 tablespoon rum

1. Purée the bananas in a blender. Whip the cream at medium-high speed until it forms high peaks. Add the powdered sugar and whip briefly until it forms soft peaks (the mixture should be light and fluffy).
2. Fold the whipped cream into the mashed banana. Carefully stir in the lemon juice, nutmeg, and rum. Spoon into parfait glasses.

Easy Italian Panna Cotta

Serves 5

COST: $0.70

Per 4-oz. serving
Calories: 260
Fat: 22g
Carbohydrates: 12g
Protein: 3g
Fiber: 0g
Sugar: 10g
Sodium: 40mg

¼ cup warm water
1 envelope unflavored vegetarian gelatin, such as agar
1½ cups heavy cream

¼ cup granulated sugar
2 teaspoons vanilla extract
¾ cup milk

1. Pour the warm water into a small bowl. Pour the gelatin over the water and let it stand 5 minutes to soften.
2. In a medium-sized saucepan, bring the cream, sugar, and vanilla extract to a boil over medium heat. Reduce heat to low and simmer for 2–3 minutes, stirring occasionally to make sure all the sugar is dissolved. Add the milk and simmer for another 2–3 minutes.
3. Remove the saucepan from the heat and stir in the softened gelatin (check to make sure the cream and milk mixture is not boiling when you add the gelatin). Stir until the gelatin is completely dissolved.
4. Pour the mixture into a bowl. Set the bowl inside another bowl filled with ice water. Cool for 15 minutes, stirring regularly. Pour the liquid into 4-ounce ramekins or custard cups and refrigerate overnight.
5. To serve, dip the bottom of each ramekin briefly in a bowl of hot water, and use a knife to cut around the bottom of the panna cotta, loosening the edges. Dry the bottom of the ramekin and invert the panna cotta onto a plate. Enjoy as is, or top with seasonal fresh fruit.

Perfect Panna Cotta

Reputed to have originated in the Piedmont district of northern Italy, *panna cotta* is Italian for "cooked cream." Traditionally, panna cotta is made with a vanilla bean, but vanilla extract makes a convenient substitute. If you want to use a vanilla bean instead, cut the bean in half lengthwise and scrape out the seeds. Add both the bean and the seeds in the saucepan with the heavy whipping cream, stirring to make sure the seeds are evenly distributed.

Banana Sundae

Serves 2

COST: $1.28

Per ½ sundae
Calories: 187
Fat: 1g
Carbohydrates: 45g
Protein: 3g
Fiber: 4g
Sugar: 29g
Sodium: 22mg

2 large bananas
¼ teaspoon ground cinnamon
1 teaspoon cornstarch
2 teaspoons pineapple juice
¼ cup Greek vanilla yogurt

¼ cup canned crushed
  pineapple
2 teaspoons liquid honey

1. Peel the bananas and slice lengthwise. Sprinkle ground cinnamon over the bananas. Mix the cornstarch into the pineapple juice and set aside.
2. In a small saucepan over medium-low heat, whisk together the yogurt, pineapple, and honey.
3. Increase heat to medium high and add the cornstarch and pineapple juice mixture, whisking constantly until thickened.
4. Spoon the mixture over the bananas. Sprinkle extra cinnamon over the top if desired.

Ⓥ Creamy Tofu Shake

Serves 2

COST: $3.15

Per 1½ cups
Calories: 255
Fat: 5g
Carbohydrates: 43g
Protein: 12g
Fiber: 3g
Sugar: 35g
Sodium: 65mg

10½ ounces soft, silken tofu
1 cup frozen, unsweetened
  blueberries
1 cup canned crushed pineapple, with juice

2 tablespoons liquid honey
½ teaspoon vanilla extract
⅓ cup soy milk

Drain any excess water from the tofu and cut into chunks. If using home-frozen blueberries instead of commercially bought frozen berries, wash before using. Process the tofu and crushed pineapple along with the pineapple juice from the can until smooth. Add the blueberries and process until smooth. Add the honey, vanilla extract, and soy milk, and process again. Chill the shake in the refrigerator until ready to serve.

Supersized Oatmeal Cookies

Yields about 12 cookies

½ cup shortening
¼ cup butter
1 cup brown sugar
1 egg
1 teaspoon vanilla extract
½ teaspoon baking soda
½ teaspoon salt

1 cup all-purpose flour
1 teaspoon ground cinnamon
1 cup quick-cooking oats
¾ cup semisweet chocolate
  chips
¼ cup chopped walnuts

1. Preheat oven to 350°F. Cream together well the shortening, butter, and brown sugar. Beat in the egg and vanilla extract.
2. Sift the baking soda and salt into the flour. Add the ground cinnamon and blend well. Mix in the shortening and sugar mixture. Stir in the oats and chocolate chips.
3. Shape 3 or 4 tablespoons of the dough into a ball about 2 inches in diameter. Place on the baking sheet, and set well apart (6 balls to a tray). Press down gently with a fork. Press a few walnut pieces in the middle, if desired.
4. Bake for 13–15 minutes or until done. Let cool. Store in an airtight container.

Ⓥ Tofu Chocolate Pudding

Serves 2

COST: $1.31

Per ½ recipe
Calories: 390
Fat: 21g
Carbohydrates: 44g
Protein: 18g
Fiber: 3g
Sugar: 29g
Sodium: 160mg

1 12-ounce block silken tofu
¼ cup cocoa powder
½ teaspoon vanilla

¼ cup natural peanut butter
¼ cup maple syrup

Process all ingredients together until smooth and creamy.

Coconut Rice Pudding

Serves 4

COST: $2.07

Per 1 cup
Calories: 448
Fat: 20g
Carbohydrates: 60g
Protein: 6g
Fiber: 3g
Sugar: 35g
Sodium: 51mg

1½ cups cooked white rice
1½ cups vanilla soy milk
1½ cups coconut milk
3 tablespoons maple syrup
2 tablespoons agave nectar

4 or 5 dates, chopped
Dash cinnamon
2 mangos, chopped

1. Combine rice, soy milk, and coconut milk over low heat. Bring to a very low simmer for 10 minutes, or until mixture starts to thicken.
2. Stir in maple syrup, agave nectar, and dates, and heat for another 2–3 minutes.
3. Allow to cool slightly before serving, to allow pudding to thicken slightly. Garnish with a dash of cinnamon fresh fruit just before serving.

Maple Date Carrot Cake

Serves 8

COST: $1.37

Per 1 slice
Calories: 394
Fat: 4g
Carbohydrates: 65g
Protein: 6g
Fiber: 4g
Sugar: 34g
Sodium: 406mg

1½ cups raisins
1⅓ cups pineapple juice
6 dates, diced
2¼ cups grated carrot
½ cup maple syrup
¼ cup applesauce
2 tablespoons oil

3 cups flour
1½ teaspoons baking soda
½ teaspoon salt
1 teaspoon cinnamon
½ teaspoon allspice or nutmeg
Egg replacer for 2 eggs

1. Preheat oven to 375°F and grease and flour a cake pan.
2. Combine the raisins with pineapple juice and allow to sit for 5–10 minutes to soften. In a separate small bowl, cover the dates with water until soft, about 10 minutes. Drain water from dates.
3. In a large mixing bowl, combine the raisins and pineapple juice, carrot, maple syrup, applesauce, oil, and dates. In a separate large bowl, combine the flour, baking soda, salt, cinnamon, and allspice or nutmeg.
4. Combine the dry ingredients with the wet ingredients, and add prepared egg replacer. Mix well.
5. Pour batter into prepared cake pan, and bake for 30 minutes or until a toothpick inserted in the center comes out clean.

Egg Substitutes

Commercial egg replacers are convenient, but ground flax meal works just as well. Whisk together 1 tablespoon flax meal with 2 tablespoons water for each "egg." Let it sit for a few minutes and you'll see why it makes such a great binder, as it quickly becomes gooey and gelatinous. If you prefer a store-bought brand of egg replacer, Ener-G Egg Replacer is the most popular, but Bob's Red Mill works quite well, too.

Ⓥ Cocoa-Nut-Coconut No-Bake Cookies

Makes 24 cookies

COST: $0.47

Per 1 cookie
Calories: 181
Fat: 8g
Carbohydrates: 25g
Protein: 4g
Fiber: 2g
Sugar: 17g
Sodium: 55mg

¼ cup vegan margarine
½ cup soy milk
2 cups sugar
⅓ cup cocoa
½ cup natural peanut butter

½ teaspoon vanilla
3 cups quick-cooking oats
½ cup walnuts, finely chopped
½ cup coconut flakes

1. Line a baking sheet with wax paper.
2. Melt the vegan margarine and soy milk together and add sugar and cocoa. Bring to a quick boil to dissolve sugar, then reduce heat to low and stir in peanut butter, just until melted.
3. Remove from heat and stir in remaining ingredients. Allow to cool slightly. Spoon about 3 table-spoons of mixture at a time onto wax paper and press lightly to form a cookie shape. Chill until firm.

Ⓥ No Egg-Replacer Chocolate Cake

Serves 8

COST: $0.37
Per 1 slice
Calories: 213
Fat: 5g
Carbohydrates: 40g
Protein: 4g
Fiber: 2g
Sugar: 19g
Sodium: 170mg

1½ cups flour
¾ cup sugar
⅓ cup cocoa powder
1 teaspoon baking soda
1 cup soy milk

1 teaspoon vanilla
¼ cup applesauce
2 tablespoons oil
1 tablespoon vinegar

1. Preheat oven to 350°F and lightly grease and flour a large cake pan.
2. In a large bowl, combine the flour, sugar, cocoa, and baking soda. In a separate small bowl, mix together the soy milk, vanilla, applesauce, oil, and vinegar.
3. Quickly mix together the dry ingredients with the wet ingredients, combining just until smooth.
4. Pour into prepared cake pan and bake for 26–28 minutes, or until toothpick or fork inserted comes out clean.

For the Perfect Vegan Cake . . .

Vegan cakes tend to be heavier and denser than regular cakes. Here are a few ways to compensate: really beat the margarine and sugar together, and make sure all the sugar is incorporated, even those pesky little bits on the side of the bowl. Also, a well-aerated margarine and sugar mix means a fluffier cake. To make sure your cake rises to perfection, get it in the oven right away to take advantage of the leavening ingredients. And of course, allow your cake to cool completely before frosting. Patience, patience!

Standard U.S./Metric
Measurement Conversions

VOLUME CONVERSIONS

U.S. Volume Measure	Metric Equivalent
⅛ teaspoon	0.5 milliliter
¼ teaspoon	1 milliliter
½ teaspoon	2 milliliters
1 teaspoon	5 milliliters
½ tablespoon	7 milliliters
1 tablespoon (3 teaspoons)	15 milliliters
2 tablespoons (1 fluid ounce)	30 milliliters
¼ cup (4 tablespoons)	60 milliliters
⅓ cup	90 milliliters
½ cup (4 fluid ounces)	125 milliliters
⅔ cup	160 milliliters
¾ cup (6 fluid ounces)	180 milliliters
1 cup (16 tablespoons)	250 milliliters
1 pint (2 cups)	500 milliliters
1 quart (4 cups)	1 liter (about)

WEIGHT CONVERSIONS

U.S. Weight Measure	Metric Equivalent
½ ounce	15 grams
1 ounce	30 grams
2 ounces	60 grams
3 ounces	85 grams
¼ pound (4 ounces)	115 grams
½ pound (8 ounces)	225 grams
¾ pound (12 ounces)	340 grams
1 pound (16 ounces)	454 grams

OVEN TEMPERATURE CONVERSIONS

Degrees Fahrenheit	Degrees Celsius
200 degrees F	95 degrees C
250 degrees F	120 degrees C
275 degrees F	135 degrees C
300 degrees F	150 degrees C
325 degrees F	160 degrees C
350 degrees F	180 degrees C
375 degrees F	190 degrees C
400 degrees F	205 degrees C
425 degrees F	220 degrees C
450 degrees F	230 degrees C

BAKING PAN SIZES

U.S.	Metric
8 × 1½ inch round baking pan	20 × 4 cm cake tin
9 × 1½ inch round baking pan	23 × 3.5 cm cake tin
1 × 7 × 1½ inch baking pan	28 × 18 × 4 cm baking tin
13 × 9 × 2 inch baking pan	30 × 20 × 5 cm baking tin
2 quart rectangular baking dish	30 × 20 × 3 cm baking tin
15 × 10 × 2 inch baking pan	30 × 25 × 2 cm baking tin (Swiss roll tin)
9 inch pie plate	22 × 4 or 23 × 4 cm pie plate
7 or 8 inch springform pan	18 or 20 cm springform or loose bottom cake tin
9 × 5 × 3 inch loaf pan	23 × 13 × 7 cm or 2 lb narrow loaf or paté tin
1½ quart casserole	1.5 liter casserole
2 quart casserole	2 liter casserole

About the Author

Nicole Cormier is a Registered Dietitian and local food enthusiast. She is an author, the founder of Delicious Living Nutrition, Inc., and the host of *Radio Brunch*. She also owns Farm Fare Market, a small health food store in Sandwich, MA. She specializes in weight-loss, diabetes, high cholesterol, family health, gastrointestinal issues, food intolerances and allergies, sports performance, and balanced healthy eating. Nicole lives in Buzzard's Bay, MA, with her partner Jim Lough, an organic farmer.

Index

215